Body Wisdom in Dialogue:

Rediscovering the Voice of the Goddess

Thomas R Flanagan and Kenneth C Bausch

Illustrated by Yuu Asano

Ongoing Emergence Press

Thomas R Flanagan and Kenneth C Bausch

Body Wisdom in Dialogue:
Rediscovering the Voice of the Goddess
Collaborative project of the Institute for 21s
Century Agoras
Illustrations by Yuu Asano

1. Body Wisdom 2. Dialogue 3. Meeting the
Other 4. Collective Consciousness

ISBN: 9780984526635

DEDICATION

This book is dedicated to fellow travelers Constantinos Doxiadis and Buckminster Fuller who – with Alexander N. Christakis and other distinguished friends – sailed the waters of the Mediterranean 50 years ago in the Delos Symposia's search of patterns, synergies, and fusions that would lead to a better world.

"What human beings need is not utopia ('no place') but entopia ('in place'), a real city which they can build, a place which satisfies the dreamer and is acceptable to the scientist, a place where the projections of the artist and the builder merge."

– Constantinos Apostolou Doxiadis

"You never change things by fighting the existing reality.

To change something, build a new model that makes the existing model obsolete"

&

"Humanity is in a 'final exam' as to whether or not it qualifies for continuance in the Universe

… I am convinced that human continuance depends entirely upon the intuitive wisdom of each and every individual … "

– R. Buckminster Fuller

ACKNOWLEDGMENTS

We want to thank Gayle Underwood, without whom this work would not have been initiated. Gayle worked heroically to help us prepare a webinar on the subject of this book for an international training course in Structured Dialogic Design which was held in Cyprus in 2011. Following this webinar we recognized that a brief synopsis of the points we were raising might find an interested readership. We also wish to thank Jackie Wasilewski both for her introduction to our illustrator, Yuu Asano, and for her work in coordinating contributions for the preface of this creative effort. Jackie has joined us in the Institute for 21st Century Agoras as our indigenous democracy expert. And finally we offer our most heartfelt thanks to Dr. Alexander N. Christakis, who devoted is full professional career to moving ancient Athenian democracy into the 21st century through Structured Dialogic Design® (SDD).

Foreword

Indigenous Traditions &
the Deep Roots of Dialogic Design

LaDonna Harris (Chair of the Board)
Americans for Indian Opportunity (AIO)
Albuquerque, New Mexico

When we at Americans for Indian Opportunity (AIO) first encountered Professor Alexander Christakis and the Structured Dialogic Design (SDD) process in the mid-1980s we were in the process of trying to find a discussion space in which Native American leaders could participate effectively along with mainstream national, state and local leaders – a special space in which everyone's perceptions of an issue could be shared and understood with respect and wisdom. At that time, these meetings were run according to mainstream conventions in which the mainstream participants dominated the discussion space. And they usually declared the meeting over before the Native American side had even begun to participate. What was missing was the means of linking wisdom across Western and Indigenous cultures.

Ancient and Post-Modern Meeting Protocols for Consensus-Building

Before connecting with Christakis and his colleagues, we at AIO had been finishing up an in depth examination of traditional Indigenous decision-making practices, all of which were consensus-based. As part of our study of Indigenous consensus-building we identified the meeting protocols, the social rules, for the way people behaved in these Indigenous meetings that enabled consensus to emerge. There were five rules:

1. Everyone affected by the problem could participate in the meeting.
2. There was an order of speaking.
3. There were no interruptions when someone was speaking.

4. There was no argumentation or debate. The point was to understand what the each person was saying.
5. The discussion went on until no one had anything else to say.

To our astonishment, these same protocols had been chosen by the Systems Scientists who assembled the SDD Process. We thought it was hugely significant that the ancient social rules for consensus-building among Indigenous hunter-gatherers and early agriculturalists were now being embraced as the social rules for consensus-building of post-modern Systems Scientists! This correspondence was surely the sign of a reemergence of a very powerful "social technology" which when combined with efficient computer assistance held great promise for addressing complex contemporary problems!

Why Are We Holding This Meeting? Arguing Positions vs. Sharing Perceptions – Diversity As A Resource

The assumption, in the Indigenous tradition, was that the reason a meeting was being held was because no one knew what to do about a problem.

If someone had known what to do, they would already be doing it, and if that approach was successful, then everyone would be following that example. So, the point of a meeting was to bring together as many different perceptions about the issue being addressed as possible so that everyone could see it more comprehensively and clearly and then, collectively, decide what needed to be done.

It was as if the "it" under discussion was in the center of a circle, and every discussant was sitting around the periphery of the circle looking at the "it," quite literally, from a different point of view.

Each perception from each point of view was, thus, considered to be a valuable contribution to understanding some aspect of the problem. And it was assumed that there would be many different perceptions depending on, among other things, the gender, age, and responsibilities of the person perceiving the issue.

There is, for instance, in the Indigenous world, the concept of "new eyes" and "old eyes" wisdom, that is the wisdom of someone looking at a problem for the first time vs. the wisdom of a person who has been looking at the problem for a long time. Both perceptions provide valuable contributions to understanding the issue at hand.

In addition, there is the understanding that *each* Tribe has its own kind of "knowledge" (and there are 500+ Tribes in the United States alone). This knowledge is based on each Tribe's origins (did they come from the stars like the Cherokee or from under the ground like the Pueblos?) and on the various ecologies they have inhabited (are they woodlands people, plains people, fishing people, etc.?) Each body of knowledge was based on careful observation of ever-changing circumstances. The Inuit are famous for their huge vocabulary regarding snow. The Comanche developed an equally rich vocabulary regarding horses (after "borrowing" them from the Spanish). And it was assumed that each body of knowledge would be different because, quite literally, it "grew up" in a different place. There was no one Truth. There were multiple truths that had to be woven together in order to understand an ever evolving larger picture of reality.

There were, thus, two major responsibilities in meetings. First, one had to speak as articulately as possible in order effectively to share one's perceptions.

One had to be able to make pictures in other people's minds. And second, one had to listen to others with one's whole mind, heart and soul so that one could understand what others were saying. All of this is in line with a Native American proverb that says, "It takes a thousand voices to tell a single story."

Honoring Different Kinds of Knowing

Not only do Indigenous traditions seek to incorporate *perceptions* from many directions, but they value contributions coming from all kinds of knowing, intuitive as well as cognitive. For example, the Oneida, one of the Tribes of the Iroquois Confederacy, consciously honor all forms of knowledge. They traditionally reminded themselves of this in the daily ritual of braiding their hair. Three strands of hair go into each braid and represented body, mind and spirit, the three sources of knowing anything, one's gut feelings and intuitions and the information from one's five senses, one's cognitive concepts and understandings and one's "channelings" from beyond the present plane of existence (Spencer, 1994).

Dialogue that honors multiple perceptions and "feeling" one's way into something just as much as "thinking" one's way results, not only in a shared language for dealing with the issue under consideration, but also in a shared *image* of the "it." Thus, the Circle of Perceptions begins to move and becomes the Spinning Medicine Wheel, the Circle Quartered by a Cross, one of the oldest human symbols, which carries many layers of esoteric meaning.

This Spinning Medicine Wheel is light years away from the Static Circle belonging to Newton's Geometry. It takes all one's faculties to manage it. Plains Indian children traditionally played a game with large hoops that they would roll across the plains by hitting them on their edges with sticks. Only in movement could the hoop balance on its rim. Observe, sense …. shift and balance.

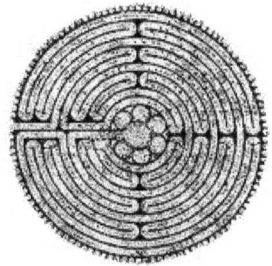

Creating an Inclusive Community Dialogue

Initially, we at AIO thought we were searching for a culturally neutral dialogue space, but we soon realized that this idea was idiotic. Humans cannot be a-cultural. We revised our search. We were looking for a culturally inclusive space – a place where we could all be heard, a place of "authentic listening," a place, not only where each person could *participate*, but where each person could make a valued *contribution* to the collective understanding of the issue at hand. In the traditions of Indigenous people, this is a sacred space. It is a space in which we can discover social reality together, because *there can always emerge another potential participant* at the edge of the dialogue circle who has been affected by the issue under consideration, there can always be another perspective that we have not yet considered.

There is an ancient Oneida teaching story called *Who Speaks for Wolf* (Spencer, 1991) that addresses this issue, that the perspective we have not yet considered may contain the key to dealing effectively with the issue facing us. Western European thought, in contrast to a search for voices, was focused on identifying the *unchanging* laws of the Universe. Laws were thought to be the *immutable* essence of the Good, the True, and the Beautiful. Indigenous thought, however, has always considered change to be an essential feature of the living Universe. A Navajo elder once stated that Human Beings get into trouble when they forget a few fundamental things:

1. There is male and female energy in this world
2. Because there are these two kinds of energy, new energy is constantly being produced.
3. For this reason, change is a fundamental feature of our world.

In Native American thought only dead things do not change, and, actually, even they change, but very slowly ... So all is process, change, balance ... all is *alive*! The World is a Living Being, Mother Earth, not a Machine.

Recognizing Dialogue Space As Sacred Space

<u>Body Wisdom in Dialogue</u> speaks of the necessity of building an environment, a "vessel," of *very highly visible respect and trust.* Indigenous People have had multiple ways of creating such spaces, especially through ceremonial means. Oneida women used to scatter goose down on the floor of the long house where an important meeting was going to take place. When the participants entered

the space their movements would cause the goose down to float in the air. This was to remind the discussants that the words spoken in that space would invisibly affect the entire community. Here at Americans for Indian Opportunity, when a new cohort of participants in our values-based Indigenous leadership development program, called the Ambassadors Program, arrives, in their very first meeting they have to answer one question: "Where did you get your Medicine?" That is, what enabled you to be present with us today? What did you have to overcome? Whom do you have to thank? This self-disclosure, by turns humorous and tragic and every emotion in between, creates a very special tone, a special kind of vulnerability and openness. It enables people to really connect as persons, persons who not only have survived, but who are now ready to create … *together.*

An Indigenous Way of Discussing Body Wisdom Is Through the 4Rs

The Indigenous approach to consensus-based problem solving is based on values that we feel are common across Indigenous communities – not only in North America, but around the world. At

AIO, we call these common underlying values <u>the 4Rs</u>:

Relationships, Responsibilities, Reciprocity and Redistribution.

These four values produce a good society where everyone and everything is *respected.* The fundamental assumption of this value set is that everyone and everything is related to each other. Second, through these Relationships our Responsibilities to each other emerge. Third, our Responsibilities are Reciprocal, that is, they are two-way, multi-way, and if we have our Relationships figured out accurately, then everyone and everything will have enough to continue and will be able to live a relatively good life. The fourth consideration is that if our present understanding of our Relationships does not result in everyone and everything having enough, then, through acts of generosity and sharing, we have to Redistribute things – both material and immaterial – including everything from basic food to highest respect – until everyone and everything has enough to continue and to be able to live a relatively good life.

The authors of <u>Body Wisdom in Dialogue</u> state that Body Wisdom "leads to growth along three vectors: self-awareness, relationship to others and relationship to environment." We see "self-awareness" as being an understanding of our *relationship to our self.* Thus, Body Wisdom is easy to understand in the context of the 4Rs. Our system of Relationships, our Relationship with ourselves, with others and with everything is an expression of the universality of Body Wisdom.

Indigenous people have internalized the reality of "constant connectedness" from ancient times to the present and have understood how to "collaborate by difference." Ancient wisdom knew that each part makes a unique contribution to the whole and that the whole is more than the sum of its parts. Body Wisdom is, in some ways, an apology for the Western glorification of thought over feelings. Many contemporary authors are making the effort to reconnect the body of the western mind with the heart of humanity. For example, consider Cathy Davidson's book, <u>Now You See It: How the Brain Science of Attention Will Transform the Way We Live, Work and Learn</u>. The authors of <u>Body Wisdom in Dialogue</u>, in addition to reconnecting their philosophy with ancient wisdom, are also pioneering the adoption of Indigenous *respect* within the complex community dialogues of our times.

CONTENTS

INTRODUCTION

This brief book will talk of philosophy, physiology, cognitive psychology, sociology and theology as they interact in modern dialogue. It aims to be entertaining and informative – playful and scholarly. Its success will be measured by the sense of the magic that grows within you. Our hope is that you will find renewed optimism for what we creatures of the earth can do together using humanity's greatest invention – dialogue.

Chapter One: Feeling and Thinking

... wonder is a flush of feeling – a sensation of
enlarging, of filling with space,
all making room for experience or revelation

– Munju Ravindra, 2010.

Dialogue is the tool through which we breathe life into higher abstractions and imagined futures – and then also the tool through which we will those futures into existence. It is a powerful tool – and yet we are still struggling to master it. Its emergence conjures up the arts in the form of storytelling, song, theater, and the subtle turn of phrases in poetry. It pushes and pulls upon our emotions. Dialogue also harnesses us into straitjackets through formal group expressions in speeches, debates and lectures. It is both driven by and also shapes our thinking. For this reason, a primer on dialogue should reasonably begin with a few thoughts about how we, as individuals and as groups, go about the magical task of thinking. To capture a phrase from William Shakespeare *"Tell me where is fancy bred, in the heart or in the head?"* In fair measure, our task is to provide you with an answer to this question. The story begins the way that our feelings touch and guide our thinking.

Abduction

Can you remember the feeling produced by TV detective stories? The investigators find a dead body and try to find out what happened and why. Some detectives examine the scene and interview possible witnesses. Someone may seem to simply drink in the scene and will have a hunch about some aspect of the scene. These are the first stages of a learning experience. It may be mysterious more than wondrous, but each little clue offers a spark of that feeling of wonder. Each clue – once recognized as feeling relevant yet also still uncertain – ignites a story line in your head. And you know that the screenwriter was stretching to produce just this effect in you. If he fails at this level, all is lost.

The great American philosopher, Charles Sanders Peirce, identified the early stages of a learning experience of mystery solving as *abductive logic.* In these stages, detectives make an observation and then develop hunches and test to see if they lead to something useful. The detectives examine possible resemblances between this case and memories of past cases. At a deeper level, these hunches may arise as intuitions derived from sensitive attention to the emotions felt in the situation and their bodily awareness. The detectives may play around with different scenarios, examining clues, and make an educated guess. As the process continues, the hunch is assessed for its "fit" – is it comfortable or does it feel stretched? Educated guesses reach for a hypothetical narrative based upon evidence found and hunches examined. This narrative provides a plausible explanation for the death. It can suggest additional clues that might be found to reinforce the narrative – or clues which if discovered would fully shatter the narrative.

Placed in a broader context of scientific discovery, Gary Shank describes the value of a good explanatory hypothesis:

> *This explanation, if it holds, allows us to summarize a lot of separate pieces of evidence, and a number of alternative scenarios, into a single coherent explanation that has the added advantage as serving as the basis for meaningful insight. That is, a good explanatory hypothesis does not just explain the obvious. It directs us toward the less obvious, and sheds light on areas once seen as unclear or unconnected.*

– Six Modes of Abduction based on Peirce's work as interpreted by Gary Shank

Some philosophers gloss over these early stages of original thinking and lump them into inductive logic. Hunches and intuitive insights can be dismissed as crude guesses rather than as seeds of discovery – theoretical problem solvers can look down on the groundwork of new discovery from presumptive heights. This happens because for those who feel they already know the way the world works, new discoveries can be seen as unnecessary assaults on their world views. It is not just the theoretician who feels this way, though. The other morning at breakfast one of our friends reacted strongly to an idea that was floating around

... "That notion pushes on me and through me like a heavy weight," he said. The new idea was threatening to him in a fashion that was deeper and more profound than an abstract concept. The new idea rattled his world view from some unseen edge. He couldn't name the source of his discomfort, but he felt the presence of the invading idea profoundly.

For Peirce, this detective-like induction works upon the good explanatory hypotheses already developed by abductive logic – whether we have a complete conscious grasp of the world view that is contained in our adductive logic or not. Induction continually tests the validity of our good and warmly held hypotheses.

The third form of logic is deduction, which accepts the hypothesis as a true theory and declares other theories, hypotheses, or assertions of fact to be false if they disagree with the theory. This can be recognized as a push-back on an observation – a reframing of an experience – an interpretation of a dream. The impulse to fit an idea into a larger world view is strong – and ideas can become bent or twisted as they are forced into place. If we reflect on our feelings as we are dealing with new ideas we can sense the amount of work that we may find ourselves doing in our efforts to fit ideas into theory, and keep our good and familiar theories alive.

As we will see in this little book, we will explore how abduction combined with body wisdom lays a firm grounding for cooperative decision making.

Deduction and Induction

The way that we think about how we use ideas is odd – at least from an ontological or developmental perspective. We think about ideas in the reverse order from which we experience them. When we formally think about our ideas, as we just mentioned, we think first about how an idea fits into a framework of other ideas. We try to fit the idea into an expectation that already has been constructed. It is not that we are lazy, but rather that we are efficient. If an explanation for a new idea can be easily offered through past experiences, we will accept that explanation. Like a free-throw shot in basketball, if the idea falls smoothly through the net, this is where it was meant to go. Throughout life, we build frameworks or nets that inform us of how the world works, and we try to sort experiences so that they fit.

We do not usually expect new ideas to be mysterious; we treat them as untidy bits of existing knowledge – something that we already know which simply has fallen off of its shelf. Some of us, of course, envision ourselves as constantly unmasking mysteries, but for most of us, this simply distracts us from the larger task of planning our futures – and it is too much work.

From an early age, we work with our personal "theory of everything" and we believe that new ideas will fit onto the shelf somewhere. As the flow of ideas intensifies with our expanding horizons, we learn to look for ideas that fit on the shelves. We "learn" to dismiss ideas that don't fit into our "theory of everything." From this vantage point, we selectively test certain ideas which cannot be ignored by making some sort of observation about the idea, and – if we are comfortable with our test – we "reshelf" the new idea. This is deductive reasoning. If our tests are not particularly demanding, then nothing will ever be new. Everything will fit. The world will hold only small mysteries, and by and large will be a safe place to sleep.

The converse process is inductive reasoning. It is real work. We first have to repress our impulse to fit ideas comfortably into our "theory of everything." We have to ignore the existence of our world view. This is hugely difficult – and for some of us may be impossible – because we must embrace an idea as a mystery. Once we start sorting through ideas which we had formerly ignored, we can be overwhelmed by them. It is like discovering that we are sitting next to a blueberry bush and suddenly discovering just how many blueberries are within arm's reach.

When we start exploring familiar and unfamiliar ideas without forcing them into our theories, we embark upon a voyage through cascades of emotion. I am not saying emotional in terms of tears and gut-busting laughter, but a rich voyage of a more subtle sort. We reach blindfolded into a box and try to guess what we are touching. We "feel" the idea in its texture, its shape, and its pliability. We search for patterns, and then search for larger patterns, seeking the hinges that will link large patterns together so that we can expand our theory of everything. Deduction is a process where our personal theory of everything rules the world. Long live the king (or queen)!

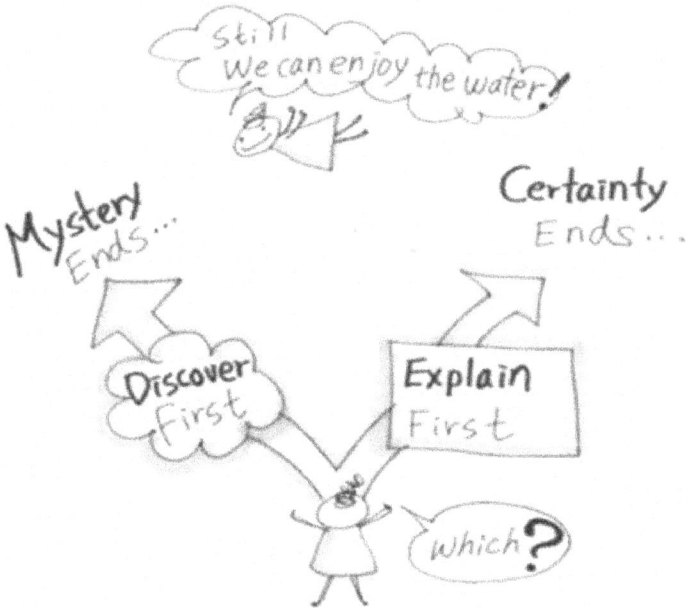

At times, we guard our personal grand theory (or world view). We want to keep it intact and durable. At other times, we want to keep our emerging understanding of the mysteries of the world alive and growing. At some points, we find a mysterious world exciting; at other points we find it to be terrifying. Is mystery adventure or threat? Do we want to discover first or explain first? This is a matter of preference, but it isn't really a choice. For those who love mysteries, mysteries do end. And for those who love certainty, certainty also ends. Sooner or later we are all left to swim with uncertainty. When this happens, this book is intended to help us enjoy the water.

Chapter Two: What is Body Wisdom?

I'm not sure I know everything that I understand.

– After Patrick Siebert's essay on Somatic Wisdom
(http://www.patsiebert.com/PDFs/somatic_wisdo
m.pdf)

*The heart has its reasons,
which the reason does not know.*

– Chinese Fortune Cookie

Most of us have no difficulty understanding the statements "Trust your feelings," or "Go with your gut." We understand that our emotions and intuitions are often more trustworthy and useful than decisions reached through laborious rationalization. This is another way of saying that we value our body wisdom.

Ever since the time of Rene Descartes, however, philosophers have had difficulty recognizing body wisdom – or perhaps the legitimacy of body wisdom as being as valid as cognitive wisdom.

The Influence of Rene Descartes

The epic schism between mind and body begins with Rene Descartes' particular need to probe into the abstract world that seems to govern our experiences in life. In 1614 at the age of 18, Rene Descartes had already studied logic, metaphysics, literature, history, science, and mathematics. And with this learning behind him he concluded that his schooling was a farce because he had only learned his own ignorance and the limitations of the way knowledge was gathered and validated. He tried once again through the study of law and once again concluded that it too was intellectually bankrupt.

For all that learning, Descartes couldn't extinguish his intellectual curiosity. He felt an urgent and growing need to understand his world in a way that his teachers and Aristotle did not. At the ripe age of 20, he retired, dropped out of sight, and began to think. He was, of course, gifted – and his methodology was unorthodox. Descartes spent half his day in bed ruminating. It is said that he invented analytic geometry while watching a fly crawling on the ceiling.

As we seek to take a few steps in Descartes shoes, we should recognize his uncharacteristic hunger for knowing life as something more than an expected outcome. Descartes was set on discovering what human life was all about – and he seemed to sense that he could do this only if he could step out of the human situation and look back into what humanity was all about. His experimental subject was himself, and his target was his sense of his own being. In dialogue with himself he asks: But what am I then? A thing which thinks. What is a thing that thinks? It is a thing which doubts, understands, [conceives], affirms, denies, wills, refuses, which also imagines and feels. Descartes peeled away at this onion skin view of humanity still seeking to find its essence – and in the experiment he shaped generations of Western metaphysics.

A Bit of Irony

It is helpful to understand Descartes voyage to fully appreciate his contribution. In 1619, while agitated with questions like how to tell who was right and who was wrong, and how to tie all this knowledge stuff together within the human equation, Descartes had a series of dreams. In one, he was startled by a noise like a bolt of lightning and dreamed that he saw a shower of sparks fill his room. In another dream, he saw himself holding a dictionary and some papers, one of which contained a poem beginning "What path shall I follow in life?" An unknown man handed him a fragment of verse containing the words "Est et Non." Then Descartes dreamed that he awoke to the fact that the shower of sparks in his room was in reality a dream, and beyond that he dreamed that he interpreted the previous dream. In the dreamed interpretation, Descartes explained to himself that the dictionary represented the future unity of science – "all the various sciences grouped together." The sheaf of poems symbolized the linkage of philosophy and wisdom. "Est et Non" signified "Truth and falsity … in human attainment and in secular sciences" (drawn from Harman, 1984).

From the perspective of body wisdom, Descartes' voyage shows how he was moved by deep internal forces to "sense" a deep personal truth. While Descartes hadn't reached bedrock for distinguishing truth from untruth, he had discovered a pathway that would lead to something that he could assert as a fundamental truth.

The Beheading

Descartes had discovered his life's work and through it has made a very large mark in our history of thought. He turned directly to beginning his *Discourse on Method.* With this work, he achieved a major breakthrough in the evolution of human thought, a paradigm shift, a new standpoint to think from. He extended the method of mathematics to all of life, demanding critical doubt at every stage of a step-by-step logical process whose goal was to uncover the secrets of nature. He had four simple rules: critical doubt; divide difficulties into as many parts as possible; begin with the simplest and work to the complex; and make complete enumerations to make sure that nothing is omitted (Descartes' process as presented In "Discourse *On Method*").

Descartes' paradigm has two fundamental parts: a method (systematic doubt) and a standpoint (that of the detached observer). He found this standpoint when he wracked his brain for some statement that he could not doubt. He found it in his thinking. While he was thinking (he reasoned) he had no doubt that he was doing the thinking. Thus his immortal dictum: **Cogito ergo sum** (I think therefore I am). He had severed the thinker from the body and the world, but no one at the time noticed the beheading.

Paradigm Thinking

The power of this particular paradigm (rigorous method and singleness of viewpoint) is revealed by the fantastic success of the natural sciences. Using the Cartesian method and viewpoint scientists transformed the world. Not only did they begin unlocking nature's secrets, they gave us power over our environment. Still, there is that troubling beheading to think about. Did Descartes accidentally disown the very thinking that produced his method? As a result, does science do the same? Good psychology today tells us that if we are to think productively about our thinking, we cannot do so as thinkers antiseptically separated from our bodies. Our thoughts originate in our bodies. Our bodies shape our thoughts.

When a new paradigm confronts and collides with an older way of thinking, we get a paradigm shift. Since the time of Aristotle, all things were connected. There was a oneness to the fabric of the universe. Descartes introduced a reductive abstraction that defined "self" as a product of thinking. For Descartes, the real world could be found in the cognitive abstractions we make of pieces of the world. This new paradigm took hold. The mind ruled the body. Feelings of right and wrong fell sway to arguments for right and wrong.

Cultural Paradigms

The path that Descartes put us on has had some powerful consequences. We might wonder: What would have followed if Descartes had found his certainty in his body; if he had declared "*I feel, therefore I am?*" He could have reasoned that he could not doubt that he had feelings. He hurt when he bumped into things; had pleasure upon hearing a song; feared in dark and unknown places; and was exhilarated in discovering his life's work. How would Western civilization have developed had it been based upon the pivotal sentence: "I feel, therefore I am?"

Try to imagine a world in which anything that you thought would be an illusion "unless" your emotions screamed out to you that it was true. The day, itself, would not exist unless you felt it in your bones. And for you, it would come into existence only when you did feel it. We couldn't say to each other "good morning" without posing confounding philosophical possibilities. Perhaps this is the world that the limbic brain itself experiences.

Perhaps this experience haunts patients with schizophrenia – a mental illness that is also called the "waking dream." Reality has no cognitive anchor, and therefore cannot be shared with others.

The point here is that it is not enough that we choose one path – we must walk both concurrently. In C. P. Snow's famous "Two Cultures" essay in 1951, he lamented a cultural divide separating human intellectual activity in the science and the arts. This is a cultural divide – it is not a division of human capacities. Yet within cultures, human capacities are either liberated or constrained. This means that cultures can force us to walk along singular paths.

Clockwork Worlds

In the 17th Century, physics moved into a powerful position guiding academic thought, and the Western World experienced a religious quandary. The world became viewed as a huge machine – accepted as of divine design, but running unattended by its own specified rules. Much of the magic of ancient beliefs began to be drained out of the daily understanding of life. Religions struggled to retain power based on beliefs, and science sought to seize power based upon stringently reasoned discoveries.

The march of mechanical thinking had begun. Descartes' rationalism, followed later in the 17th century by Isaac Newton's laws of motion, set us upon a course of empirical rationalism that culminated in the 19th century's notion of the "clockwork universe," where the world was conceived as run entirely on abstract logical laws. This does not mean that everyone agreed, but rather that the powers in place at the time celebrated the mechanical view of the world for its pragmatic predictability. Cannon ball trajectories were, after all, difficult to argue against.

Cultural Frictions

It took time before the resistance that was voiced against this march of mechanical thinking gained legitimacy. Baruch Spinoza was an early critic of Descartes' division of body and mind. He argued (c.1670) that no one has ever

> *laid down limits to the power of the body; that is, no one has as yet been taught by experience what the body can accomplish solely by the laws of nature. ...Thus, when men say that this or that physical action has its origin in the mind, which latter has dominion over the body, they are using words without meaning, or are confessing in specious phraseology that they are ignorant of the cause of said action*

> – in Frederick Pollock 1880, appendix D

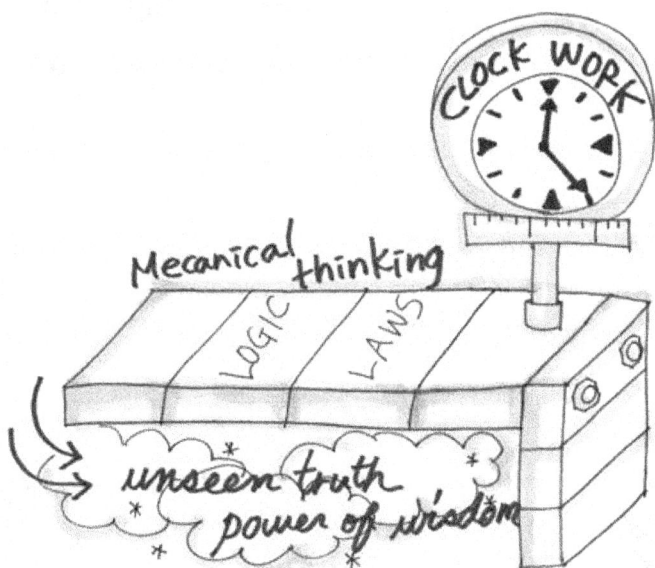

Poets especially felt Descartes' misstep. The gap between the core of science and the core of art expanded. William Blake at the end of the 17th century foresaw this arid rationalism ahead and lamented for the impoverished universe which was to be Newton's legacy. Blake's short verse is:

> *May God us keep*
> *From simple vision*
> *And Newton's sleep*

Blake, from his position in the culture of the arts, was lamenting Newton's reduction of the universe into geometry and his neglect of the world of the unconscious.

In later centuries, society itself became more complex as the paradigms of art and the paradigms of science co-existed and presented competing views on how we should lead our lives. They differed on how situations should be perceived and how decisions should be made. As the waters of complexity rose, individuals were coerced into clinging tightly to the cultural ways that most strongly impacted their lives. Cultures of discovering and cultures of believing grinded alongside each other creating heat from their friction.

Rediscovery of Uncertainty

Eventually, certainty itself gave way. In the 20th century, science moved away from the idea of a stable world that we can observe from an objective point of view and can describe with linear explanations. In the physical sciences, the Newtonian world view was consigned for use in "normal" situations only. Einstein's relativity theories and Heisenberg's uncertainty principle dragged us securely in the middle of an uncertain physical reality. The physical impossibility of completely understanding a single point in the universe destroys our illusions of objectivity.

Heisenberg's Uncertainty Principle [loosely] states that it is impossible to know both the exact position and the exact velocity of an atomic particle at the same time. We are forced to choose from among mutually exclusive perspectives to make definitive individual statements. We are forced to consider many individual situations concurrently, and accept individual reality as a probabilistic outcome. The world no longer can be broken infinitely down into reductive pieces and yield trusted understandings.

It has taken us over a century, but philosophers and scientists are finally awakening from Newton's sleep. The real mysteries lie within the interactions among things. Today we are still beginning to realize that visions from many viewpoints are required for understanding reality, especially social reality. We can be whole again. We can value our personal feelings about the world and how it works.

The myths of William Blake's time may not resonate for us now. They were based upon the big story of a paternal creator in constant interaction with his angels and men. Goodness was measured as obedience to hierarchical authority.

Today we are experiencing what in 1996 Gerard de Zeeuw called "*third phase science.*" The three phases of science are: first, the study of things that exist apart from us (such as astronomy); second, the study of things with which we personally interact and may change as we are making our discoveries (such as psychology and anthropology); and third, the study of things that must be understood from multiple sciences (such as social systems and sustainability). At this time in our history, we are coming to recognize that all complex social reality is a third phase science phenomenon.

Postmodern Uncertainty

To add to the depth of modern complexity, we now also recognize that all knowledge is incomplete. Our new myths about situations in the world are based upon a big story of non-linear complex relationships. To some extent they revitalize ancient myths, such as the relationships that the Greek Gods enacted. The veil that has kept our emotions isolated from our thoughts is rent asunder. When we were comfortably sleeping in our machine age, we fashioned our gods as expert engineers. When our engineers design our machines, there is no function called the mysterious X. There is no reservoir of unpredicted results that is actually included as part of the machine. Now that we are confronted with the reality that our machines are continuously evolving, and our worlds are infinitely mysterious. Our machines themselves must include provisions for the mysterious X.

Psychologists tell us that the mysterious X function is an essential factor of the psyche. That it is an essential part of that animal limbic brain that is at the core of the emotions of pleasure and panic in us all. Maybe it is no coincidence that our mechanical view of the world has been forced to make peace with its mysterious nature at the same time that our psychological science has come to accept the presence of a mysterious X factor within and among us.

The "unknown" is an inescapable part of any understanding. Einstein expressed this idea in the quip *"as the circle of light increases so does the circumference of darkness around it."* In the conscious realm, even our clearly recognized emotions carry an unperceived shadow of additional feelings. We may or may not be able to name and understand essential mysteries; we are, however, probably tuned to feel their presence if we open ourselves up to sense them. On an individual basis, some of us are cats that like to land immediately on our feet and others are acrobats that like to linger and dance on the air. When we are comfortable exploring mystery together we are dancing.

Perception of Mystery Linked with Sense of Awe

The universe itself is an overarching source for sensing the Mysterious X. In its timeless vastness, the universe is awe inspiring – it can take our breath away even as it yields up some of its mystery. We each have our own personal experience of awe in the face of our universe – we can sense its fathomless, unearthly wisdom, and we can deal with this mystery in no other way than to feel it resonate with our body wisdom, our emotions, and our intuition. The gift of humility in the presence of the Mysterious X – in any form with which we encounter it – beckons us as eternal learners. In the twilight at the edge of time, what we know as unarguable truth is infinitely small, and what we are capable of feeling as unfolding mystery is beyond measure.

Chapter Three: Where Is the Inner Conversation?

"I would say to you: the truth can only be truth to each man and to each woman according to their inner understanding

— Ramadahn
(http://www.meilach.com/spiritual/ramadahn/ram
ad5.htm)

The Call of Mystery in Times of Crisis

At this crucial point of human history, we may feel paralyzed by the rush of immense global events. Reflection can relieve this paralysis by showing us an informed, progressive, and pragmatic path to the future. At the edge of history and the dawn of our futures, we are always more than what we think. The deep roots of our belief are guided by primordial sensations that we can't outgrow. We all have "gut feelings." Sometimes we just know that we have to do something, and not until later does our mind realize that our gut was right. In a similar way, we sometimes receive a subtle summons to explore an idea or a path of action. We can be led also by other impulses; however, with reflection we can sense the difference between an impulse and a calling.

As you read the prior paragraph, we ask you to reflect on how you are feeling about the concept of *Body Wisdom*. Are you feeling happily creative or perhaps guardedly skeptical? Does the term body wisdom have a special meaning for you? Have you sensed that reflective dialogue was an emotional experience as well as a cognitive experience? As we introduce and discuss this topic, try to be mindful of your "emotional pulse." The essence of what we will be presenting is that our inner feelings are a part of the mechanism through which our body wisdom will speak to our conscious mind.

From the dawn of time, the mystery of the universe has resonated within us. The call isn't a call voiced in riddles of the mind. The call beckons from greater depths. The mystery calls out from an untouchable void. Its haunting song rattles us with unanswered questions. And together, or as lonely spirits, we are summoned to answer.

The vastness of life's mysteries can be likened to the vastness of the night sky. Our ancestors imagined epic adventures that populate empty spaces in the sky. These adventures are recorded in tales that symbolically speak to our spirits. We, too, can feel the dark sky as frightening unless we see it as speckled with flecks of hopeful light. Night's shadow masks lurking dangers, and our minds invent our wished-for defenses. From the very darkness, hope springs up to us. When we will it to do so, the night sky carries our experiences and wishes into the neutral and unforgiving theater of life. This night sky was a powerful motivator for our forebears.

What then is this universal summoning that stirs us to create myths? What inner prayer calls us to focus on moments of profound mystery? What is the dark inner force that compels us to write stories into the night sky? Do these stories tell us something important? Jungian psychologists call this territory the "numinous" – the hunting ground of the psyche. It is – to our best knowledge – a uniquely human territory.

We each enter into the numinous in our time and in our own way. The voyage can shape our approach to life. In what feels to be just a few short years ago, my son at age eight and I went for a swim at midnight beneath a canopy of stars. The water was cool yet not cold. The air was still yet not lifeless. The distant calls of loons vibrated across the membrane of the lake's surface. And an aurora of starlight cascaded upon the night. After an initial ten minutes of splashing our presence into the lake's being, my son's eyes turned upward. And in the silence I could feel the awe in this exhaled whisper – "*Wow!*." I knew from the sound of his voice that he had been touched by a moment that would shape him in ways that he could not yet comprehend. I knew that he felt a presence, and that presence forced from him a simple yet all telling response. I also knew that in the long seconds that would follow, he would experience an unstoppable urge to talk about the moment. He would call upon his voice in an effort to express the inexpressible. And in the common ground between experiencing and sharing he found a phrase "*How cool is that!*" I am not sure I know exactly what the words were saying but I was certain that I shared his meaning. "*Yeah, how cool is that*" I answered.

We write into our personal skies with the words and feelings that the mysteries of life evoke in us. Again, we ask, why is this so? What deeper wisdom forces us to express our feelings in the form of ideas? And then why is it that such an experience – when shared – can so powerfully unite us in a sense of common voyage? We share an urgent need to communicate such experience with others. And we feel relief in the perceived success of sharing our deepest realizations. Why is this?

Simplistically we might say that we are social animals and need to coordinate our socialization through communications. Then we might backcast from our theory and assert that this compulsion exists to drive us forward to achieving our communicative imperative. But this is a circular argument. Our deductive logic puts the cart before the horse. Somehow we have become social animals from some status which was – in great probability – way back in our evolution. Some compulsion drove us and still drives us to communicate. Over the eons, we refined the social experience and adapted it as a means to organize our collective actions. Emotion has, we argue, been an essential part of the experience.

Too much of an experience can leave us numb to the perception of the experience. A fish swimming in water, knows only water and thus not only is unable to imagine a world without water but also cannot sense the water that it swims in. So too we as humans swimming in a sea of emotions may not sense the waters we are continually traveling through. Our emotional experiences and emotional knowledge carries us – it signals what is familiar and trusted, what is exotic and may not be trustworthy, and what seems to be irrelevant and might be safely (and wisely?) ignored. The interplay between raw feeling and thoughtful expression in our decision making processes may be fully inseparable. We may never be capable of making a decision which we could "prove" to be purely cognitive and utterly divorced from our emotional milieu. Even thinking machines – should we create them – would be founded upon programs initially crafted through human experiences.

Raw feelings do become explicitly encoded into abstract, cognitive expression in some very visible ways. They can be crystallized into symbolic thoughts somewhat like the way that energy itself becomes crystallized into matter. If we split open a crystal thought, we might release a cascade of subatomic feelings – an explosion of feelings. If we bend, snap, or distort the meaning of a word, we might evoke wrath or dissipate the tension through humor.

Words themselves are mere placeholders for meanings that come into and move about the world. Words are symbolic expressions of understandings that we want to capture and share. The symbolic expressions are close to the substance of our lives, and yet they also are only the medium through which our life energies move. Our emergence into a world of symbolic language is an essential part of the human experience. Our ability to evoke body wisdom and encode it into language provides us with essential skills for navigating our collective lives.

The Neurobiology of Mind

Inspirations come in various guises. Albert Einstein said *"I very rarely think in words at all. A thought comes, and I may try to express it in words afterwards"* (Wertheimer, 1959, p. 213). Einstein also said:

> *The words of language do not seem to play any role in my mechanism of thought. The*

psychical entities which seem to serve as elements of thoughts are certain signs and more or less clear images which can be 'voluntarily' reproduced and combined... The above mentioned elements are, in my case, of a visual and some of a muscular type.

– Hadamard, 1945, pp.142-3

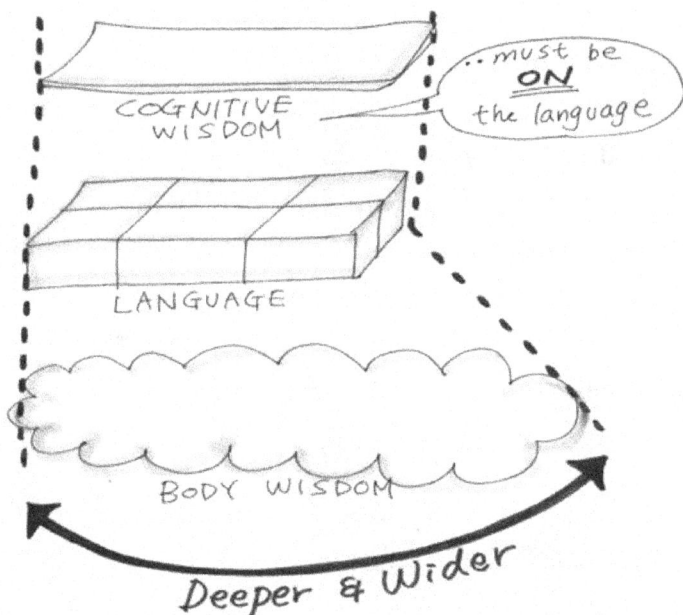

This concept – and the philosophical discourse related to it – is thoroughly discussed in *Body*

Wisdom, a philosophical book published by Ken in 2010.

Great things can spring from humble beginnings. It seems reasonable to suggest that some form of instinctual and adaptive knowledge predated the emergence of language. Neuropsychologists can correlate regions of the brain associated with neurochemical "reward systems" as playing important roles in learning and memory. This suggests a biological linkage between emotions and understandings. An ancient and deep brain structure, the limbic system – sometimes called the "lizard brain" – has a survival value which remains a part of us today. The limbic system is highly emotional and rapidly reactive. This means that the limbic brain can "feel" a response before a conscious mind can "express" it. Our biological legacies are an important part of our body wisdom.

Individual Reflection, Anticipation and Collective Discernment

Reflective practice in philosophy and theology is based upon sensing something which we may be about to understand. This is the felt presence of an idea that we cannot yet name. In many ways, body wisdom is superior to cognitive wisdom, which relies upon language. The body creates language when we are infants. Language never captures anything without leaving a remainder unsaid. Yet we need language so that we can order our cognitive knowledge. If we deal with situations on the basis of pure cognitive wisdom and logic, we leave ourselves open to the deficiencies of language. True wisdom comes when we blend our cognitive powers with a keen sensitivity to our body's signals.

Body wisdom is a progressive feeling. It beckons us from the core or our being. It pushes us to progress along three vectors of growth: self-awareness, relationship with others, and relationship to our environment.

Right now, as you are reading these words, can you feel yourself asking *"what might be coming next?"* Can you feel this anticipation? This expectancy signals that something is coming, even if you have no sense for what is the next focus in the page ahead? The sense of anticipation that something is waiting in the mist ahead is just the point that we are trying to make here. If you can stretch out this moment – hold it in time and look at it – you will see that your body is calling out to your mind saying '*Wait, wait! There may be something in the forest ahead that makes a difference.*'

Body wisdom guides us to listen, to ask, and to desire an opportunity to speak – or to remain silent. You can override your body wisdom urges when you recognize them, but without sensing them, they will silently and rapidly steer your thoughts and actions.

Ouroboros and Origins of Cyclic Chemical Structures

Primordial forces lift solutions from the subconscious. The figure below shows an ancient symbol, the Ouroboros (or Uroborus) depicting a serpent or dragon eating its own tail. It comes from the Greek words "oura" meaning "tail" and "borus" meaning "eating", thus "he who eats the tail." Symbolically, it represents a continuous cycle – suggesting the abstract concept of infinity – a situation that never ends. The circle seems to carry this meaning in many cultures. It may have a single origin in history or may reflect a more general expression of an inner feeling for the abstract concept of infinity. It is an image that shapes thoughts.

The Ourobous image came to the assistance of a German chemist (Friedrich August Kekulé) at a time when he was burdened with a profound mystery. The mystery involved discovering how to make sense of a chemical observation that benzene had six carbon atoms, but the known rules of chemistry at that time could not explain how these atoms were assembled into a compound. The mystery haunted Kekulé, and. as he slept. the unresolved problem crept into his dreams. Within the dream state, Kekulé stopped thinking with his prescribed set of cognitive chemical rules and began to think in imagery. In his own words in 1865, Kekulé said:

> *There I sat and wrote in my notebook, but it did not proceed well, my mind was elsewhere. I turned the chair to the fireplace and fell half asleep. Again the atoms gamboled before my eyes. Smaller groups this time kept modestly to the background. My mind's eyes, trained by visions of a similar kind, now distinguished larger formations of various shapes. Long rows, in many ways more densely joined; everything in movement, winding and turning like snakes. And look, what was that? One snake*

grabbed its own tail, and mockingly the shape whirled before my eyes. As if struck by lightning I awoke. I spent the rest of the night working out the consequences.

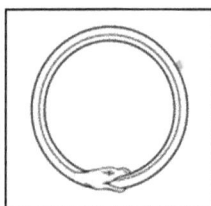

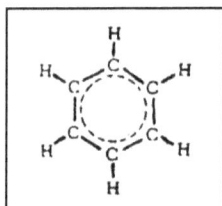

From Ouroboros to cyclic chemistry

What is remarkable about this story is how a part of a chemist's mind unmistakably used images – not words – to express a relationship that was beyond the language of the chemist's cognitive mind. Cyclic organic chemicals had never been imagined previously. We can consider this an example of creative inspiration, but then we still have the challenge of guessing from what source such inspiration has emerged. We see this unvoiced, deep wisdom as part of what we are calling body wisdom. The images are the outputs. The psyche is the drawing board. A complex mix of sources pours inputs into a deep pool of inner wisdom – some inputs pass through to conscious thought.

Entering into Consciousness

Impressions take shape as ideas. Envision a waterspout lifting shapeless water into an elevated funnel. Such an image expresses the creative process. Our focused attention hovers over our unconscious mind and draws shapeless meaning from our unconscious waters – translating that meaning into a structure of words. Body wisdom draws meaning from our unconscious and urges us to find an expression for it. The wisdom that is expressed is the fuel of our social lives. It is mined from our subconscious waters and put into motion through subconscious insistence and conscious art.

Fortunately, we tend to give some measure of warning before we confront each other head on with the full force of our subconscious ruminations. In deep dialogue, you and I are both actively connected to our individual unconscious depths and we sense that this is where we are both standing. We generate a transcendent understanding and sustain it through our sharing of words. This kind of dialogue is worlds superior to the chit chat that is a mere bantering of words without connecting them to deep personal experience. We do, however, need both deep and also casual communication. Without casual communication, we would risk profound philosophical and emotional entanglements whenever we said hello to each other.

Because ideas must flow in a fluid state, it can take a while before they are fully formed. If we presume that we know the meaning that we are about to hear from another person, we might entirely miss that meaning. Meaning has to be discovered. It isn't hatched fully grown and armed like the goddess Athena springing from the head of Zeus. Body wisdom is the progressive force that gives life to the meanings we share. It beckons us from the core or our being. It pushes us to progress along three vectors of growth: self-awareness, relationship with others, and relationship to our environment (which is the "stuff" we most commonly talk about).

This reasoning implies an ordered or sequential flow of proto-meaning from the subconscious to meaning within the conscious. The triggers for this movement of body wisdom into cognitive wisdom can be external sensory stimuli from the physical world or shared abstract understandings from our cognitive world. While the pathway might be certain, the voyage is not. The glimpses of understandings that enter the cognitive mind are both powerful and a fragile emergence. If we are too overpowered with sensory stimuli or an emotionally charged situation, we can repress the appearance of body wisdom.

Yes, there is a playful process called "brainstorming" which tosses all of the salad of our conscious mind into a bowl and stirs it briskly. This approach hopes that by stirring cognitive wisdom rapidly enough, new compositions of matter will emerge – and the new matter will drag previously unvoiced wisdom with it. More often than not, however, a feeding frenzy of words downplays our body wisdom and draws it away in the rush to cognitive wisdom; and – upon subsequent reflection – it can leave us feeling that brainstorming was fun yet not deeply fulfilling for us. We may feel that a "decision" reached through brainstorming has robbed us from the relief we were seeking for problems that we sensed at deeper levels. The point we are making is that creativity comes in multiple forms, and that some forms of creativity draw upon body wisdom while others repress body wisdom.

Awe and Sense-making

Body wisdom prepares us to deal with obscure and mystical forces. Without being glib about it, the universe is factually awesome. It overwhelms us with mysteries of scale and process. We are one with this awe as we allow ourselves to experience it. It stirs our minds. It has a comforting and haunting quality. A mysterious feeling of comfort and an equally mysterious sense of threat evoke the awareness of a powerful presence. To deny the presence, we must deny the feelings. But the feelings are deeply sensed and embedded in the very fabric of our psyche.

Our psyche itself is not just a dark night of pleasures and dreads; it is a deep well of unspoken wisdom. Within our depths we sense an infinite innerness that is echoed in the infinite outer-ness of the night sky. We can tap the resonance between the unknowable depths within each of us and the unknowable vastness that surrounds us all. And the flexing and stretching between both infinities compels us to discover each other through symbol and language. The discovery process is a matter of abductive and inductive logic, a logic of sensing connections, testing connections, finding connections. Sense-making is, in its essence, a matter of finding connections. It is not a process of arguing for consistency, but rather an experience of feeling the consistency.

At our very core, we are one with the universe. And in that universal union we are one with each other. Sharing the night sky together – or sharing any awesome natural experience together – we can feel our connectedness. The way in which we are connected provides a third dimension in addition to what is within us and what is beyond us. This dimension of what is between us opens infinite possibilities for our exploration. We explore our connections to each other through successive approximations of shared feelings and shared thoughts – including our individual aspirations and dreads. Our interconnections constitute an explorable infinity. All that is within us, and all that is beyond us, and all that is among us defines three dimensions along infinite vectors. We move through time and space in this triangulation. As we negotiate our understanding or our position, we discover where we are by knowing who we are. Without the capacity for this discovery, we are lost and adrift on a mooring-less night sky.

Horses, bears, cats, and dogs – of course – are creatures of the same universe. Their lives are guided by their own sense of knowing – their own senses of inner feelings and their own awareness of imminent moments. In their evolution, they negotiate their own form of peace between feeling and knowing. They display behaviors which we interpret as acts of care for each other and their offspring. They survive in what we perceive to be difficult situations. In rare instances – and in only some species – symbolic language emerges where individuals can speak to and share abstract concepts with each other. Dogs learn human words – the word "bone" comes to represent a real bone. Humans learn cat sounds and gestures. A "tail touch" becomes a shared and comforting greeting. We can sometime sense pets as fellow spirits and even sense the land as a living being (i.e., Gaia, the primordial Earth-goddess in ancient Greek religion).

Given that what we do not know is always going to be a lot larger than what we can possibly know, we might wonder about our chauvinism in talking of "subhuman" life forms. We presuppose that, if given a choice, a whale or dolphin would prefer to rise to the status of human existence. Maybe, maybe not. Something in us may sense that the realities experienced behind the eyes of non-human beings are similar to our own. We may feel that the capacities of human life hint of divine inspiration, but we should realize that our own high-flown aspirations and the experience of other animals emerge from shared waters. We see evidence that linkages between body wisdom, cognitive wisdom, and social connection are not unique to our own species. In our individual lives the linkage is an emergent property. We are presumptive in assuming to know when and where such linkages may exist beyond our own direct experiences.

In comparison with other mammals, human infants are born "prematurely." They require considerably more care and protection than herd animals or aquatic mammals which are able to orient and move with others shortly after birth. As infants, however, we do learn and adapt very much in the manner of our animal cousins. We are much attuned to our situations, even before we can be said to "understand" those situations. Developmental psychology describes the infant's experience as being "one with its mother." The sense of this bond is intimate and very, very real for the infant. A common cause of an infant's insistent cries is the even momentary absence of its mother. The sensation of separation feels like a theft of part of itself. Jungian psychology recognizes the fear of being isolated as a fundamental foreboding of the psyche. The infant's psychic existence is exposed, unguarded, and undefended. Wounds at this stage can endure for a lifetime. These are formative years, and they are comprised of moments that are pre-formed in our bodies.

In its hopeful rush toward truth, science often tells us that we can understand our biological history if we question the way an infant matures. We can ask, what is an infant's life like in its comparative simplicity? What form of felt emptiness summons forth language in the infant? What softly felt void does an infant seek to fill with words? Is the creative emptiness first felt as the anguish of separation? We can also ask, when does an infant discover that it is safe to be separate from its mother. What enables this discovery?

The Ontogeny of Cognitive Wisdom

Sigmund Freud stumbled upon answers to these questions while watching his grandson playing in a crib. The boy had been troubled for weeks. He would cry loudly whenever his mother left him and stop when she returned. One day Freud watched the boy as he was playing with a spool tied to a string. The spool was hanging over the side of the crib. The boy was holding onto the other end of the string. As the boy lowered the spool so that he could not see it, he said "Gone (Fort)." As he pulled it back up, he said "Here (Da)." He kept repeating this process.

Freud perceived that in this "Fort/Da" experience, the boy had discovered the power of language to stand for abstract things – situations that could not be understood from experiencing them alone. Freud subsequently observed that the boy no longer cried when his mother left the room. The boy could now have his mother's presence by just imagining and naming her.

With this discovery of language, the boy was no longer an infant. He now had the world opened for his investigation. He entered the world of cognitive reason. Language opened up the world of consciousness.

This opening of consciousness happens for all of us. Language opens for us all our philosophy and science. The poetry of Homer gives expression to our deep yearnings while the troubling questions of Socrates challenge our facile explanations. One philosopher gave expression to his deep body wisdom; the other philosopher challenges us to dig deeply into our own body wisdom. Generations later, Newton constructed an elegant way to express some of the laws of the infinite physical universe; and subsequently, quantum scientists confronted paradoxes that throw back into question the very notion of fixed scientific truth. Such cycling of knowing and discovering over the ages is one gift of language.

Language does have at least one nagging side effect. With the development of language we no longer have our unquestioned feeling of the unity that we had experienced with our mothers and sensed with the universe. We yearn for that wholeness of unity. In the gap, we are torn between our desire for individual accomplishment and our need for community – a unity with nature, each other, and with our bodily selves. Freud's own life and quest for unity led him to propose a theory of Eros and Thanatos based upon just this tension.

Another side effect of language is the opium power of words. Once we have learned how to mask the pain that we sense through our body wisdom, we can immunize ourselves from body wisdom's pinpricks with an ever increasing medicine chest of words. We can label a scary thought, and thereby place it in a box – and hide the box in a closet – and lock the door – then even walk away from the house; we may go too far for our own good. What the conscious mind locks up in a closet, the subconscious mind continues to watch. While we can deny feeling body wisdom, we cannot deny its power to act through us.

Conscious Awareness of the Presence of Body Wisdom

After the mind creates language, does body wisdom lose its power? Of course not! It remains tuned to the universe.

We channel its wisdom and power by attending to the sometimes obscure messages sent to us by our unconscious. As we attend to our moods, feelings, and intuitions, we can use language to make our body wisdom explicit. The insights garnered from body wisdom give shape and power to our linguistic constructions of the universe.

Jungian psychologists tell us that body wisdom, in the form of the psyche, is embedded deep within us and communicates by pounding on the membrane that separates the conscious from the deeply subconscious. The psyche is the essence of feeling, not sensory yet sensual. It is a beast that is bold and timid – dodging in shadows and poking out from darkness. The psyche is the inner eye upon the universe. It works in quiet moments and evokes the creative mind to express feelings that are too deep for words to fathom. It speaks of harmonies and discords, of voids and dense compressions, of eternal pasts and infinite futures. It speaks in archetypes from our living culture that it drags into its lair.

It is important to recognize that while we do sleep consciously, the psyche never sleeps. Even as we are fully awake, the psyche too is mindfully building up its store of body wisdom. It strikes chords of emotion in approval or in alarm all day long – and well into the night. It is like a shadow that we can see only from the corner of our eye or a rainbow that we can see only when the light is just right. It is there always, sensing and reporting the mysteries that please and disturb the fragile ancient animal within us. But when the time is right – when we laugh and when we sing – when we mourn and when we grieve – or when we pull ourselves up in fright or dread, body wisdom joins forces with the cognitive wisdom and they assert that "we see a truth."

There are two special ways to access our deep wells of body wisdom. We can meditate and we can dialogue. As we meditate, we open ourselves to our unvoiced truths. As we dialogue, we feel our body wisdom and bring this unconscious wisdom to others in our constantly tested use of words. We choose the words that "feel" appropriate to our sensed body wisdom. And through these shared words and ideas, we express our body wisdom – reaffirming its sense of truth or confronting its possible misconceptions.

In meditating, one steps off that mental treadmill where we continually chase ideas in endless pursuit. This can be done in a variety of ways: prayer; Zen, Tibetan, and Transcendental meditation; the Whirling Dervish dance; etc. We "distract" or "detach" ourselves from the world of ideas and attend to our body in its physical unity with the universe. To be individual and to be infinite at the same moment is another type of awesome experience. The experience calms the psyche and opens us to universal tunes and rhythms. Working at this level we approach the Zen ideal of *wu wei*, the principle of no effort. There is effort required of course, but with practice we can construct avenues to travel the world of cognitive wisdom and have body wisdom resources appear for us. When we work from this level, we sense a vast untapped and always incompletely experienced presence. We move into and through the world of cognitive wisdom with a richer sense of serenity and confidence.

Stilling the mind with the strength of body wisdom gives mind space to dig deeper and reach further in its unending quest for meaning. Our minds quest for ideas that fit together, fill gaps, and manage the cognitive load as we move more deeply into the unknown. When we ignore body wisdom, our mind's forward progress is stalled. We may feel stifled or in retreat. Without body wisdom's guidance, we can get mired in conflicting currents of words that signify nothing. When we are overloaded with ideas or otherwise feel oppressed, we either curl up inwardly or we strike out defensively – with words and ideas, or with other resources. Body wisdom can give us the courage to search for safe pathways through complex worlds.

The complexity of the universe is given to us as a resource to strengthen our body wisdom and enrich our cognitive wisdom, but this gift can at times seem beyond our individual reach. It is for this reason that we have invented dialogue as a means of reaching for understanding together. In this reaching we share a common purpose and confidence founded in body wisdom, which enhances our capacity to learn together. Dialogue stimulates and lubricates our mutual quest for pathways through complexity. In our common purpose, we construct shared language, and through shared language, we share meaning. In dialogue, shared meaning leads to shared wisdom. The wisdom is one part cognitive wisdom and an equal measure of body wisdom. The way cognitive words are used echoes our body wisdom. They are not separable.

Chapter Four: Meeting the Other – How does Dialogue Connect Us?

*Americans and British are one people
separated only by a common language.*

– Attributed to Sir Winston Churchill

Diagnostic Dialogue

David Bohm lived much of his life as a physicist. He worked with empirical rules of nature that govern the interaction of material forces. He sensed that forces existed beyond interactions, and worked to name them. Bohm felt a special attraction to a certain aspect of dialogue. He felt he could 'take the temperature of a community' by observing its conversations. The method is diagnostic, but not prognostic. That is to say, it is not directed to a specific outcome; it merely senses and understands how the community is sharing in the moment. What happens next requires a community decision.

In effect, Bohm views conversation as a sandbox for building bridges and castles together, or not. His notion of conversation did not set capacity-building as a required outcome for conversation. His insight was that by watching how we play together in the sandbox, we can understand something about what our communities may need. We can see the interplay of body wisdom and cognitive wisdom in their natural setting. Such a sight is, of course, not always a pretty state of affairs.

Conversation, and this could include some internal conversations with our better-considered selves, are sometimes simply pleasantries. We can see each other and see ourselves in the mirror of conversation, and compliment ourselves on our good looks. Such dialogues provide commentaries that happen as we walk along a wooded path. They are a means for body wisdom and cognitive wisdom to socialize with each other. They are rehearsals for things to come. In contrast, directed dialogue constructs a situation where body wisdom and cognitive wisdom must learn to work together and play nicely. Directed dialogue anticipates an outcome – even if the expected outcome is not identifiable up front.

Back to Bohm. Watching folks misbehave in dialogue is instructive. We observe that productive dialogue can be derailed by our very capacity to share feelings. We can observe specific behaviors that suppress the voices of others. For example, speakers who are impassioned to speak are not at that moment prepared to listen. Impassioned speakers tend to speak loudly and rapidly, and so prevent others from injecting ideas into their train of thought. And a dialogue that fosters rapid reaction and reply ends up extinguishing reflection. When these things happen in dialogue, individuals broadcast their ideas – crowd the airwaves with the presence of voices – and yet the messages can go unheard or misunderstood. In situations where individuals feel they are not heard, they can become angry in their need to respond. As emotion intensifies – and as frustrations mount – the very desire to speak and be heard can dissipate. Speaking and being heard are, of course, quite different. Free-form dialogue does present an opportunity for communicating; it does not, however, guarantee communication.

To provide greater assurance that speakers might be genuinely heard, – and realizing the necessity for communication – humanity has invented additional forms of dialogue. Dialogue first became facilitated (i.e., with Robert's Rules of Order) and then further became structured (i.e., with Structured Dialogic Design). In the process, the street brawl of emotions and thoughts that rise up when large groups confront complex situations became transformed into an ordered means of regaining a sense of communal oneness.

Linking Body Wisdom and Cognitive Wisdom

Dialogue at its roots is a search for meaning "through spoken words" wherein we open our defenses and exchange probing ideas together in search of shared understanding. It is a collective application of abductive logic – and this can be difficult for the uninitiated. In collective exploration for shared truths, we comingle body wisdom and cognitive wisdom and thereby discover newer and richer forms of meaning at both the individual and collective level. Under appropriate conditions, the well chosen or spontaneous words that we utter can summon our unconscious wisdom into a form of wisdom that we can share.

In these collective abductive explorations, words are essential yet also not sufficient. This is because words themselves have only an associated meaning; they simply behave as markers for a personal meaning that lies beneath them. Words which are charged with deep meaning for one individual cannot reliably transfer a complex wisdom to someone who has had a different experience of life. Groups must agree to discover the words – the language – that is appropriate for sharing their wisdom. Words that conjure up resonating forms of body wisdom in others can help groups we can groups build and share a collective body wisdom. With successive touches, words can sculpt meanings which takes shape in the form of understandings in the minds of others.

Of course, as we mentioned, there are familiar ways to use language for making conversations purposeful without the use of collective abductive enquiry. Speeches, for example, are given to present a point of view which then may be opened for some measure of comment. Debates are held to determine winner and loser in a contest of ideas where "correct" answers are assumed to be known in advance. Theater provides a vicarious experience of a conversation in which specific chunks of body wisdom are hauled before us and given life to resonate with our felt experiences. Actors thereby become the personification of feelings. Staged situations become the crucible for forging new wisdom through actions of actors. The audience merges with the theater in an experience of oneness. And, sometimes, the experience and the sense of theater stay with the audience as the audience carries its newfound wisdom toward its reflective consideration of the broader world. Every experience with spoken words is not an end in itself; some are just preparations for a dialogue or conversational experience that is yet to come. It is for this reason that we all should be aware that different forms of oral expression belie different intentions. Speeches inform, train or mobilize. Debates construct win-lose contests. Theater pulls body wisdom into learning situations. Conversation builds communication skills. But we share most authentically when conversation steps up to become a real exploratory dialogue – when our pleasantries turn to explorations of intentions and meanings. The starting point for such dialogue is the deep presumption that we actually can – and must – learn from each other.

COGNITIVE WISDOM

BODY WISDOM

In the view that we are offering, dialogue is an exploration which is headed toward an anticipated destination, but the destination must be discovered by naming and understanding landmarks along the way. The landmarks need to be jointly explored so that they are interpreted consistently to be sure that the entire group arrives at the same destination together.

The ways that ideas and meanings come together leave footprints in both our cognitive wisdom and our body wisdom. In this sense, verbal exchanges call to us from our distinct pathways and invite us to journey together. Many variables affect the quality of our travels. With differing levels of passion, differing levels of conversational skill, differing levels of perceived understanding, differing levels of presumed authority, differing levels of shared identity, and differing levels of situational complexity, we have a range of linguistic approaches that can serve us. Any directed dialogue approach needs to address environmental realities along with the internal principles that link body wisdom and cognitive wisdom. Some approaches do this more effectively and more reliably than other approaches.

Tapping Deeply into Body Wisdom

Tapping into body wisdom is a natural skill, and yet like any human skill, performance can be enhanced with practice. There are two privileged ways to tap inner wisdom: meditation and dialogue. The solitary practice of meditation brings us into a deeper individual experience of oneness while dialogue opens up the opportunity for a collective experience of oneness. We focus on the generative and regenerative power of dialogue because of its power for shared discovery. In dialogue leading to shared oneness, we lower our defenses in order to explore meaning together. We also go beyond our customary ways of thinking. We go beyond small talk and explore uncertainties in our relationships with each other, with the world, and even with ourselves.

All of us have probably had our mood lifted when someone authentically listens to us. We might also have felt a lift in listening to a friend. We might even have experienced a special bond while listening to someone as we were simultaneously being heard. This deep mutual sharing is what holds couples and close friends together. Such deep sharing reveals the gift and power of body wisdom as the essence of community.

Consider your own recent experiences with verbal interactions in large groups. What were they like for you? Was there a keynote speaker? Was it a lecture? Did you spend a lot of time listening, and perhaps too little time expressing ideas that were bouncing around in your mind? What many people call "dialogue" these days frequently leaves people feeling frustrated.

In a group, when a speaker says something that doesn't feel right, body wisdom urges us to engage in dialogue to better understand what the speaker really means. In small groups, it is easy to ask for a clarification. In larger groups, the dialogue often moves too quickly, and before ideas are fully clarified, the discussion moves on. After a while the accumulated unanswered questions make it difficult to hold on to the meanings that are being expressed. We come to sense that we are missing important understandings. Our confidence in the process and its outcomes declines. We begin to lose hope that our participation really matters.

On the other hand, maybe the "dialogue" is intended as an inspirational motivator instead of an exchange and recombination of meaning. Maybe the audience is a chorus and the understanding is really the understanding that stands at the podium. Maybe the speech is called a dialogue because the speaker is seeking an engaged sharing of body wisdom alone – sharing an experience, but holding back from explicitly sharing the varied meanings that we might attach to that experience. Maybe the performance art of "the dialogue" is its primary purpose. In such extreme cases, we become more tuned to the energy of our body wisdom than to understanding our cognitive wisdom – and we are out of balance. Even if the experience is fun at the moment, in the light of the next day, how will we look back on the experience? Will we be trapped in the myth that "dialogue" experiences like these are all we can hope for - a flood of ideas sweeping across cognitive landscapes or a chorus of cheers emerging from the hopeful folds of body wisdom?

We assert that a productive dialogue requires that body wisdom and cognitive wisdom are brought into harmony and held in balance.

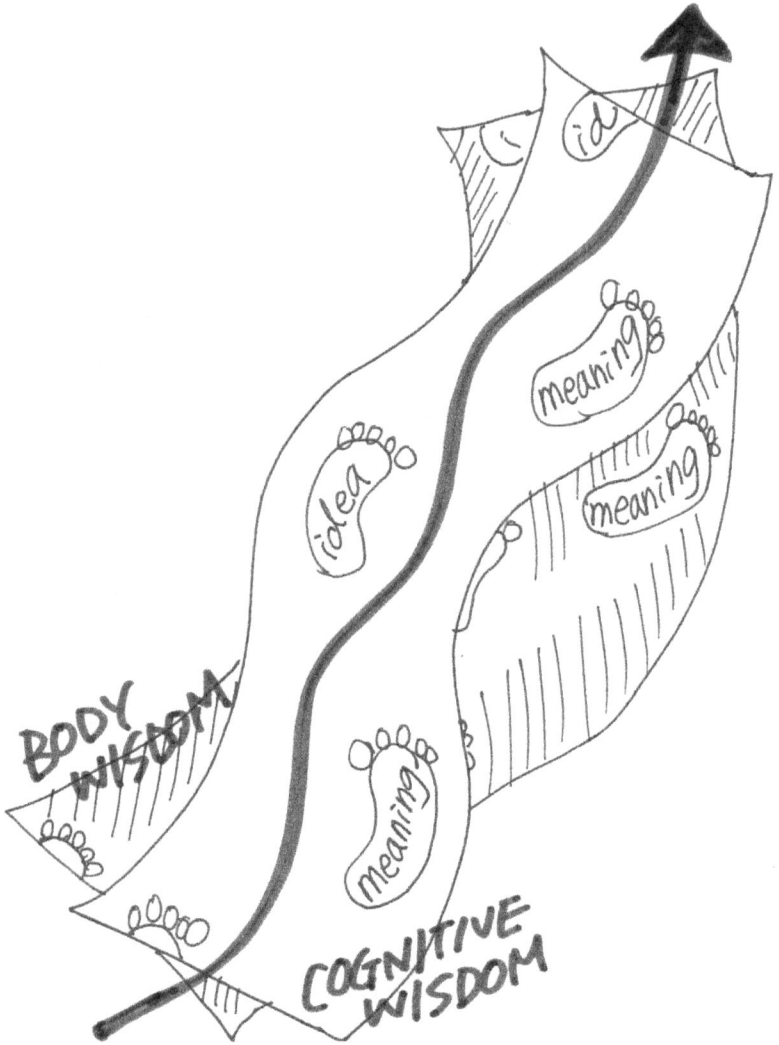

Chapter Five: Becoming One –
What is Collective Consciousness?

*The core political values of our free society are so
deeply embedded in our collective consciousness that
only a few malcontents,
lunatics generally, ever dare to threaten them.*

– attributed to John McCain

*The world we are experiencing today is the result of
our collective consciousness, and if we want a new
world, each of us must start taking responsibility for
helping create it.*

– Rosemary Fillmore Rhea,
from New Thought for a New Millennium

The Consciousness of a Culture

Because the human mind – individually and collectively – is finite, we have invented ways to capture meaning in the spaces that surround us. Cave paintings hold stories and reflect their meanings back to us. Epic poems have the same effect. We continue to paint meaning into our surroundings and "institutionalize" meaning into our culture. For some of us, some meanings have passed a critical test for immortality, and thus become excluded from collective exploration.

We feel that it is important to make a distinction between the artifacts of learning – a statement of some form – from the process of learning. If learning is continuous, then the process of learning must also be ongoing. We cannot become slaves to what we had once felt was a discovered essential truth of the universe. Yes, cultural cohesion is important because it defines a playing field and allows us individually and collectively to set out certain expectations. But the encoded messages painted on the cave walls of our culture are always only a fragment of the wisdom of our cultures. We cannot afford to mistake a picture of an antelope with the reality of an antelope. We must work within our collective cultural expressions if we are to learn from each other; we cannot, however, enslave ourselves to the understandings that were expressed with only the information that was available in the past. A cultural consciousness which imposes imperial fiats upon us crushes individual and collective body wisdom.

One of the barriers that must be lifted to free our spirits and to link our body wisdom with our cognitive wisdom is the barrier that insists we have no right to reinvestigate our cultural foundations. Indeed, if we the people lack such a right, who in the world has this right – and how does the world learn to adjust to changing times? Capturing a new cultural consciousness is a long and winding road, and if we wait to be given permission to start this voyage, we may be denied the voyage altogether.

Structured Dialogue for Group Expression

Who speaks for the people? Sometimes a specific member of a group will claim that they and they alone have the power to interpret the sacred landmarks that are discovered during a dialogue. This assertion of power pushes some members of the community out of the discourse. As a result the discourse becomes so corrupted that it ceases to be a dialogue at all. The point is that discourse is a fragile tonic. It can fortify or it can poison. It can create feelings of community or it can shatter them. It can enrich understandings, transform them, or negate them. Discourse, conversation, and dialogue, come to us in varied forms. Rules of fair play are needed because some weaknesses of human nature lead some individuals to presume that their wisdom is superior to the wisdom of others.

It is good to have a sense of the "rules" upfront because dialogue spontaneously emerges in the special "space" that comes into existence when couples or groups of friends meet. Spontaneous dialogue seldom emerges between strangers or competitors in confusing situations. Conversation may emerge, but dialogue waits off stage in the wings. In complex or in unfamiliar situations, dialogue needs to be cultivated. The cultivation needs to follow some rather simple implicit or explicit rules. The default position for starting is to scan the group and see if anyone of the group is a "rule bringer." A rule bringer will be a trusted member of the community who can assure participants are heard. If a rule bringer is not present, then the group works from memory of prior examples.

Rules should be only as complex as they need to be. One simple rule is that while a speaker is speaking, others wait and listen – for a "reasonable" span of time. The reasonable time limit frees the group from long-winded tirades, filibusters, and circumlocutions. And there is also a natural period of silence after someone speaks ... sometime only a moment. If the silence is too short, the group loses the opportunity to reflect upon what was just said. Talking "over" another speakers reflective moments is not so different as speaking at the same time that they are speaking. How long should a reflective moment be? We can tell by the eye-contact that we make if those among us are still processing a thought. Our body language tells us when we are engaging our body wisdom.

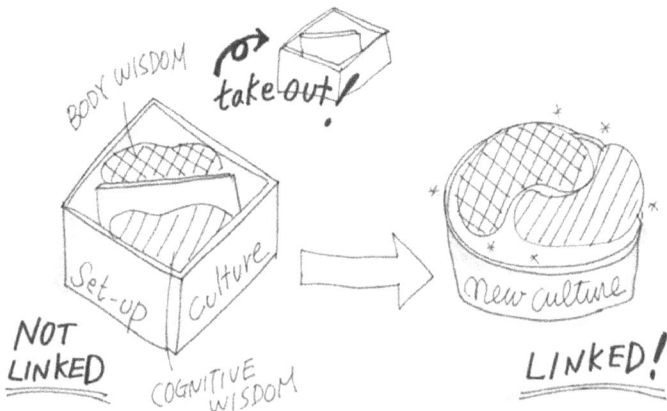

Individual orations should be limited in time to keep people from forgetting points made early in a speech. Reflective time can be crushed by an original speaker as well as by a follow on speaker. Complex ideas need to be "chunked." The listeners need to be in control so that the "chunking" is done correctly. And to do this, the speaker needs to be sensitive to the listeners' signals that they are chunking effectively. Chunking is an interesting phenomenon. We experience it when we hear "words" and "complete idea" without attending to the fine structure of the sound of letters within a word or a string of words within a sentence. We chunk sounds into works, and we chunk words into meaningful expressions. We need time to gather and reassemble chunks of meaning if we are trying to share deep knowledge.

These simple rules of fair play are intuitive to many in the sandbox, but not to all. For many, the rules will simply "feel" right. For individuals who have had their voice suppressed in their lives, or who may have suppressed the voice of others, these rules may not be sensed as a natural part of body wisdom. In such situations, effective rules need to be learned and adopted as norms for the group. For some groups, the learning will require a skilled rule bringer. In complex situations, where significant amounts of chunking and discovery of meaning is required, the rule bringer will also need to introduce some information management tools.

In complex situations, structured dialogue is needed to support group efforts by cataloguing, tracking, and assembling meaning. Structured Dialogic Design (SDD) is a specific approach that was devised to cultivate inclusive understanding among unfamiliar individuals who need to explore complex spaces (for details on this approach see www.GlobalAgoras.org). SDD combines empirically discovered and scientifically validated rules of dialogue from diverse sources which, together, reliably build a climate of mutual trust, respect, and, eventually, compassion. The approach brings body wisdom and its passions into harmony with cognitive explorations. It enforces the rule that people listen to each other first without judgment and refrain from criticism, thus addressing complexity by avoiding the consequences of unexamined crosstalk.

Crosstalk

Crosstalk is an expression of a certain type of body wisdom, so it is worth explaining what is going on when a dialogue is rippled and riddled with crosstalk. In cybernetics, as also in electronics and even harmonics, crosstalk is a phenomenon that occurs when a "signal" – let us say "a statement consisting of a specific set of words" – travels along its intended pathway but also jumps onto another, related channel and begins to move along that pathway as well. In musical composition, this might equate to "resonance" where a vibration from certain instruments might cause the strings on a piano to hum.

The sense of harmony can be an alluring call. The "presumed meaning" in the signal (the string of words) can create a sense that a tight fit exists – or that a sharp discord exists. The risk here is that if a signal (an idea expressed with a string of words) is not specifically explored, a false meaning can be carried via crosstalk. To simulate the sound of very deep notes in church organs which lack the extremely long pipes needed for directly producing such note, a set of upper harmonic notes are played which cause listeners to mentally reconstruct the "unheard" deep tone. When we mix meaning with misunderstanding we erode the quality of our learning. We can imagine hearing what has not been said.

People can and do use the same words, and yet talk about different meanings. For this reason, SDD slows the pace of the dialogue by specifically asking the group if meanings feel really clear. This clarification testing process forestalls unwarranted assumptions of understanding. Clarification is limited to the task of "understanding" the ideas alone. Expressions of disagreement are not permitted during clarification so that all meanings can be heard without bias. Disagreements can be voiced, of course, but only after participants are really certain that they understand each other. In this fashion, SDD engages – and then calms – our urges to assume that we know what each other is thinking. This assures us that we have the time it takes to fully clarify what we do mean. Managing this task is both art and science, and as we will discuss shortly, it is also part of an integrated vision of how body wisdom and cognitive wisdom interact in productive complex problem-solving dialogues.

Building Environments of Trust and Respect

Trust is the foundation for linking Body Wisdom and Cognitive Wisdom. Trust can be cultivated in a variety of ways. In dialogue, trust is fostered when participants demonstrate a commitment to respect the ideas that are shared. Such a dialogue becomes a liberating voyage.

All structured dialogues begin with the selection of where to go. This involves a bit of magic, actually. In our experiences, there is a sort of "kindling" effect that draws attention to a topic. A few tiny twigs of an idea seem to ignite, and these twigs happen to light up others. The idea that something needs to be discussed starts to rise to the surface. The idea might move to the surface as a felt opportunity, a sensed threat, or a deep longing. It might find voice as a "prospecting question" – something like *"what is the source of the feeling that we are dealing with? Is it something so vast, complex and immobilizing that we just can't seem to see it?"* Some community members might be able to strongly push an idea upward, while other community members might hope to talk about something else. At some point, an intuitive read of the situation is achieved by those who have the privilege or the responsibility to call the community together. They voice the idea that needs to be discussed and they invite or command the community to gather. In conversations, the initial idea may drift, blend into, and shift with other ideas. In a structured dialogue, the idea will remain central to the exchange of thoughts. The central idea will be presented and protected as "the trigger question," and complex meaning will be unfolded, sorted, and assembled as responses to that specific question. In this way, structured dialogue is a focused dialogue that begins by getting participant agreement on a carefully crafted "trigger question."

When the trigger question is presented, members of the community respond by feeling their reactions to it. If it feels "right," then it is accepted. If it feels unclear, then it is discussed to assure clarity. Typically a trigger question resonates profoundly with a diverse set of the "theories of everything" that participants bring into a complex problem discussion. To avoid introducing a trigger question that is outright rejected by a community, preparations are done to assess not only the readiness of the community to engage the subject, but also sensitivities about how the question is phrased.

Once a focused dialogue's trigger question is accepted, participants respond to the question first by writing down their ideas or factors to consider. They are asked to express the salient ideas, the ones that rise to the surface of their minds. Salient ideas are upwellings, pushed to the front of the mind by body wisdom. If asked why we have chosen them, we may come up with some *ad hoc* rationale from our cognitive wisdom, but the more profound truth is that they are the things that we feel are most important to say in response to the trigger question. By silently writing and working independently, we each reflectively tap into our individual pools of body wisdom and begin to bring our wisdom forward into the dialogue. The formal process used in SDD is called the Nominal Group Technique (NGT). It traces its origins to the work of Andre Delbecq and colleagues almost a half century ago.

As a relevant side note, Andre Delbecq is a professor at Santa Clara University where he teaches courses that integrate spirituality into contemporary business leadership. It seems that the reverence induced in NGT sessions resonates with progressive spiritual themes. This profound reverence also stirs in the communal discernment practice in the Jesuit order, which is similar to the idea gathering phase of NGT. NGT can be seen as an interpretation of what St. Ignatius Loyola called gathering the "motions of the soul." In this practice, people speak only when they are sensitive to their thoughts, imaginings, emotions, inclinations, desires, feelings, repulsions, and attractions. This is also a cornerstone in the practices of the Quaker faith.

As participants strive to collect their responses to the trigger question, they may find themselves in unfamiliar verbal territory. They may struggle to express something they feel in their hearts. In the ensuing dialogue to clarify meaning, participants understand that others are also struggling to express deeper meanings. They come to sense the imminence of shared, deeper meanings. They see that they learn from each other and glimpse the prospect of learning deep truths and gaining power through deeper understanding. When participants perceive this opportunity, they can find themselves behaving in respectful – dare we say reverent –

fashions. The sensation of being in the presence of the powerful collective wisdom can evoke a feeling of infinite possibilities through shared learning and collaboration.

As the observations/answers and the clarifications proceed, one can feel tension evaporate within the room. The uneasiness of being constrained in an unfamiliar approach transitions into a sense of newfound community. People become trusting and express their feelings because they sense that they are being heard and that by being heard they are contributing to the emergence of the group's understanding. People listen to each other and understand where the others are coming from. Respect is transformed into a degree of trust. That part of us that is the keeper of body wisdom is given a warm reception for its wishes to share.

Shaping a Shared Wisdom through Dialogue

New meaning emerges from effective participation in complex dialogue. In a group, and even a small group, an individual who is desperate to be heard is not yet ready to listen. Listening requires a special frame of mind and urgency isn't it. Yet urgency cannot be denied; it must be relieved if participants are to really listen to each other. SDD manages urgency by having participants "name" and "post" their ideas for all to see. Ideas which are surfaced in NGT are acknowledged in sequential round-robin fashion, and posted so that everyone recognizes that a specific participant is introducing a specific idea. An urgent idea and a sense of ownership of that idea is rapidly established, and – in this way – everyone gets a placeholder for their urgent responses onto the menu and recognizes that they will be given the opportunity to be heard by the group as the dialogue continues. Each person frames their individual idea in his or her own words and has sole ownership of the authentic meaning of that specific idea.

As students in our early classroom experiences, we seek a teacher's attention by raising our hands high when we know an answer, or we avoid detection by ducking our heads when we do not know the answer. In this seeking or hiding from attention we sense body wisdom's rules for competition and for survival. A similar dynamic is at work in group discussions where participants are fighting to be heard – or seeking to avoid imagined embarrassment. It is an old classroom convention among the information "haves" and "have-nots." Unless a teacher is in touch with the needs of all learners, the quick and keenly expressive students will dominate in the information contest over the more reflective and more exploratory learners. The traditional classroom of the early 21st century, with its centralized authority of right answers and wrong answers, is a poor model for learning through dialogue. In our early classrooms, information – not meaning or understanding – was the currency of exchange. We were being trained – we were not being asked to contribute to new understandings. Anxiety and urgency can be fostered in training environments, and explorations of meaning beyond or beneath the core information can be constrained. Students complying with standardized testing mandates are drilled in an essential march forward, often without a required opportunity or encouragement for looking sideways.

Brainstorming

Another part of group learning that deserves a moment of consideration is the process of "brainstorming." Here again, a feeding frenzy of expressions is fostered in the hope that the rapid collision of information in the form of ideas will generate fresh perspectives and foster discovery of hidden meanings. Ideas are tossed against each other, and crosstalk twists and bends meanings with results that rapidly skim but cannot deeply mine creative exploration. Brainstorming does not search the depths of a complex problem. The process is fun – for some (think of those who raise their hands rapidly in the classroom competitions of youth or in the boardrooms of later life).

For groups that are so inclined, and for problems that are not deeply rooted in complexity, the approach is fun and has its place. It is possible to play on a basketball team and never shoot the ball. It is possible to be in a brainstorming session and never score your point.

Because brainstorming is popularly entrenched in facilitation practices, we need to be clear about our concerns. Brainstorming misses the input of thoughtful, reflective contributors who don't do well in this arena. Their deeper reflections do not receive due consideration because they are blitzed by the rapid addition of other folk's enthusiastic ideas. Their original meanings are "distorted" and "dismissed" as the freight train moves onward to its destination. Their feelings, too, are likely to be marginalized.

Yes, we should agree that the good of the whole is nobler than the pleasure of the individual; however the pleasure of the majority need not be either *the good of the whole* or *the pleasure of the individual.* Brainstorming takes us to some point where the group stops tossing more ideas into the soup. It is the point when the popcorn stops popping. It is a point where a collective exhaustion or accepted disinterest takes over. If exchanging ideas in this "quickie" fashion were as rapturous or embracing as an act of love, one can certainly find some participants who if asked "was it good for you" would answer in the affirmative. Others, whose love might be deeper or more complex than this process allows, would disagree.

Brainstorming risks making the silent portion of a group feel unproductive and unfulfilled. Without setting itself out as dry and curmudgeonly, structured dialogic design specifically avoids the confusion of confabulating ideas that result from the brainstorming exercise. Structured design is guided by the principle that problem solving through dialogue begins on a foundation of shared individual understanding of the problem. Participants construct a shared vocabulary and a consensual understanding of their situation, the situation they desire, the obstacles to their desired situation, and the actions they will take to overcome those obstacles.

The point here is that body wisdom is used for different effects in different forms of dialogue. Dialogue approaches which focus on recitation or on spontaneous, uplifting expression can pull us away from deep listening. We do have simple desires to talk and be heard that can be costly when repressed

While most of us enjoy seeing the impact that we create with our words, this pleasure is distinct from the deep yearning that we share to be heard. Listening is about the greatest honor we can give each other. The awareness that "we will be authentically heard" which emerges early in SDD sessions sets the stage for deep learning.

Chapter Six: Seasons of Humanity – Can We Balance Asking with Telling?

In the early Greek philosophers,
the psyche tended to be identified
with whatever had been selected
as the animating principle of the universe.

– Reese, 1991, p. 466

Reese's comment invites us to explore the meaning behind the myth of the beautiful and troubled *Psyche* in her relations with the goddess *Aphrodite* and Aphrodite's son *Eros*. We see Psyche's struggle as being metaphorically aligned with the emergence of a new presence through the resources of body wisdom.

Ancient Insights through Divine Stories

It is important not to mistake an icon for a god. Many dialogues, including SDD, result in a durable and reproducible product of some form. Groups that use SDD construct a "map." The map displays the core structure of a complex situation and a narrative about the origins and propagation of effects in that complex situation. It is a record of the group's strongly agreed understanding of its situation and its understanding of options for addressing its situation. This map, however, is just an artifact; it does not represent the living presence of Psyche. The map does not radiate the vitality of the goddess but rather tracks her footsetps. In fact, too strong a focus on the map can confuse others. While the map has special meaning because it reminds members of the group that created it of their interactions, learning and agreements, it can be simplistically interpreted as only a reasoned conclusion by others who did not participate in its creation. And this is the point: a conclusion – regardless of how radiant its inspiration may have been – can only carry a way a slice of the experience itself. For us, Psyche represents the power of the search for new understanding – her mythic story is an artifact.

Let's start with the myth of Psyche, Aphrodite, and Eros

The Fragile Beginning of New Ideas

The quality of emerging inner power (that of Psyche) includes reflecting, recognizing greater powers, accepting limitations, but tempered with resolution, and measured consistency. This power is open, active, and constantly learning. It is a posture in which one places oneself at the threshold and is discovering new ways of being. Established inner power (that of Aphrodite) includes confidence, pride, and power over the emergence of new inner wisdom. In dialogue, Aphrodite is the old guard and Psyche is the upstart. Psyche cannot hope to defeat or change Aphrodite, and Aphrodite has the power to deny or kill Psyche. But because of Psyche's allure upon others, Aphrodite cannot kill Psyche outright. Aphrodite's goal is to drive Psyche to despair and to thereby repress the emergence of new inner wisdoms.

In the following interpretive account, Aphrodite represents the old guard as the distant and commanding powerful *god.* Psyche is the upstart seeking to find connectedness and represents the emerging goddess. As we explore this myth, consider how a group might use dialogue to discover connections and how such a discovery embodies the spirit of Psyche.

In the ordinary course of events, when people seek guidance, they would heed the authoritative voice of Aphrodite who would ordain the legitimate thoughts of the group. Psyche will offer different advice. She will beg the group to discover its own thoughts. Usually Aphrodite will carry the day. If the group is provided with just the right question, however, the voice of the group will reach beyond the declarations of Aphrodite and speak through the fragile collective and interconnected voice of Psyche.

An Interpretation of Psyche and Aphrodite

Here is an account of the myth of the contest between Psyche and Aphrodite. Psyche (like all new ideas) has a rough early start. While her sisters seem to be on a path toward marriage and happy-ever-after, Psyche – who came into being from coalesced dew drops – was thought to be so fantastically beautiful that she was too great a beauty to be courted, and thus was not. Psyche was a beautiful idea that just didn't fit in, so Psyche came to feel the loneliness of inner imprisonment. In addition, her beauty bothered Aphrodite, who was instantly and dangerously jealous. Aphrodite – even as another feminine goddess – had no desire to save her, and Psyche's lament became "no one understands me" – the poor beautiful new idea.

Psyche's father, a king (of course), was embarrassed that the youngest of his three daughters seemed destined to go un-courted and unmarried, and as a creature of his time he reached externally for an answer to an internal problem. The oracle that the King approaches, not to any surprise, is dominated by the old inner wisdom of Aphrodite. The oracle's prophecy is that the new idea must die. Psyche is to "marry death." The king is not to kill his daughter outright, but rather to take this new idea and chain it to a rock in a remote place where death will overtake it. It will be a dreadful death in large part because it will take an unrealized life.

In matters of internal affairs, kings and gods alike yield to the overt expressions of Aphrodite's vain wisdoms. The King chained his daughter to a remote rock and abandoned her. Psyche's despair darkened into remorse. She accepted marriage into death as a threshold through which she – her inner self – could enter into a new sphere of consciousness. She herself was the portal. As a new idea, Psyche was a portal to a new way of seeing the world. She threatened the old ways and suffered their onslaughts as she sought to find her future home. And so Psyche awaited her own death. The myth, of course, cannot stop here without killing off all hope for an emergent future. She is already on stage, and the audience is not satisfied with this perfunctory execution.

Aphrodite is appropriately complex herself. She resents Psyche's rise to power, yet she also doesn't want to have any maiden (new idea) die at the hands of men (that is, anyone who commands external actions). Aphrodite has influence on the outcome through the marriage arranged to death, but does not want the will of another being to cause the death. Stepping forward, Aphrodite calls her son (who is the god of love) and influences him to act upon her will even if it is contrary to his own. Aphrodite's son (called Eros or Amor or, yes, Cupid) cannot deny his mother. Aphrodite wants to have Psyche fall in love with Cupid and thereby to be seduced by the intoxicating and blinding power of love. In this way, the maiden of the new idea will die as she is transformed into the lover of Cupid. That part of Psyche which is dangerous will have been tamed and can then be forgotten. Once again, the audience doesn't want this simple death for Psyche either, and so the myth goes further.

As Cupid is carrying out his mother's wisdom, he gazes directly on Psyche, and – even though the myth cannot claim that Cupid understands Psyche – the beauty of the new idea he senses before him distracts him. Cupid accidentally pricks himself on his own arrow of love and decides at once that he shall marry Psyche. New ideas can have this effect on the easily influenced. They can be courted too briefly and adopted too quickly when the power of love overtakes the power of wisdom. But the audience, of course, is intrigued. Nothing good can come of THIS, they sense.

Cupid has Psyche carried from the rock to a paradise where Cupid and Psyche become one. Psyche is now both less and more in her personification of a new idea. It is an uncertain time. Her voice is mingled with the voice of another. Her inner understandings are tempered by feelings that come to her through another. She has to make sense of her new situation in the world. Her old individual idea has died, and in its wake the self that was that old, new idea, takes on new dimensions. Psyche, who was born as one new idea, has evolved into yet another new idea. She is as beautiful as always, but now she is different too. Psyche has learned. The audience can imagine as they will the subtle and deep ways in which Psyche has learned more about the world and about her situation. The myth, however, is more explicit.

Cupid as a god with power over external affairs is, we are led to understand, unaware of any inner change within Psyche. Moreover, he specifically tells Psyche that he doesn't want her doing her internal discovery things on him. Psyche is prohibited from "looking upon" Cupid.

In dialogue, a speaker cannot be certain that the ideas that she or he has expressed have affected a predicted transformation in the ideas that are carried by others. There is an exchange that is an incomplete knowing. In a poetic exchange, words from a speaker are vessels into which listeners pour their own meanings. When artfully crafted, poetry summons related – though never identical – meanings, and a group re-experiences a time that they had never spent together before. Poetry and sacred text summon lonely pasts into a shared presence, and offer a different promise for the future. Psyche's sense of loneliness is not cured, but hope has been discovered.

The quest of infinite closeness with others is never fully realized. Psyche is bound to the meaning of a new inner idea that was born into her and that she alone has carried. Now, at this stage in the story, the meaning beneath the idea has evolved and she is transformed. Psyche is still alone with the infinite closeness of her new idea, and now she is also bound to Cupid with earthly closeness.

Cupid, on his own part, as the externally focused god, cannot fully understand Psyche, and we are led to understand that he instinctively fears her powers for inner understanding. Cupid, as both a god and an idea, does not want to yield himself up for examination. To shield himself, he prohibits Psyche from looking directly upon him and enquiring into any of his ways. He insists that he is to remain a mystery unto her. Psyche agrees, but the audience senses that this is not Psyche's way and that sooner or later she will have to look upon and into Cupid. The risk to Cupid, of course, is the fear that someday Psyche may come to realize that – love notwithstanding – Cupid is not enough for her. Cupid is in love and fears rejection by Psyche, not sensing his own inner capacities for parallel transformation.

So Psyche finds she is intellectually alone once again, within her marriage. Her inner expression cries out for voice. Cupid hasn't the ears with which to hear her. Without sharing her inner ideas, Psyche is still chained to that rock.

With the passing of time, Psyche's sisters are drawn by concern and curiosity over the fate of the idea that was their sister. It seems that ideas which are repressed are not always easily forgotten. Psyche's community of sisters called out to her, not to retrieve her, but to assess her fate. When Psyche tells Cupid that she has been contacted by the community, Cupid responds with dread, telling Psyche that this community can cause her great danger. Cupid adds threats onto his warning to Psyche. The community of mortal sisters is to be feared, even by a god who has fallen in love with one of them.

Well, Psyche agrees, but the community is persistent. The myth doesn't tell us why the community is so insistent to get to Psyche's new story. Perhaps we are all presumed to understand that a primordial hunger exists for new stories. Psyche's new story now is elevated way beyond a new idea. She has things to say that others know they cannot guess. The belief in an emerging inner wisdom in Psyche is a compelling lure to the community. They return again and again. To Cupid's dismay, he eventually yields to their persistence and allows the sisters to come for a visit (dialogue).

As the audience anticipates, the community of sisters pushes Psyche for details. When confronted with Cupid's rule that Psyche cannot look upon him, they conjure up mean rumors with which to compel Psyche to break Cupid's rule. As the myth continues, Cupid's fear and the audience's expectation are confirmed. Psyche turns her inquiry upon Cupid and breaks his rule. Psyche discovers that her husband is the god of love himself, but the joy of her discovery provides little happiness.

Cupid is angry and hurt, and flies home to his mother. Psyche is abandoned on the broken earth – wiser, but decidedly less happy. Her sisters pushed her to learn, but discovering the truth was painful. For the audience, the same pain can be felt in different ways and in different degrees. Learning can shatter balances that hold relationships together. Experiences will teach some individuals that learning isn't necessarily good. The audience is confronted with a sophisticated riddle regarding what is right and what is wrong.

Myths, of course, do not allow audiences to guess about their resolutions. Psyche's struggle is not about her relationship with Cupid, but rather with her relationship with Aphrodite. The collision of the inward goddess and the outward god comes to little happy consequence on its own. It is only their ultimate happy reconciliation that can endure.

Psyche is stronger for her wounds. Aphrodite, however, is unassailable in her power. Cupid had done his best to keep Psyche happy and ignorant, but he failed. The proverbial ball is in Psyche's court. Psyche is profoundly unhappy and, once again, the notion of further conscious transformation (though self-chosen drowning this time) presents itself to Psyche. Where an externally focused god might turn toward acts of killing for transformation to higher heroic levels, an internally focused goddess contemplates acts of dying to transform to new and deeper reflective levels. To act upon this, Psyche must summon her inner resolve, which is the very foundation of her goddess strength.

As Psyche approaches the river, she is met by the god Pan – the external wildness and near madness that is beyond oneself. Pan is on hand to help. His goal is to drive Psyche outside of herself. He compels voice, and it is through voice, that people pull themselves up from within – even if imperfectly. Some individuals approach dialogue as Psyche approaches the river as a confrontation with forces that will ultimately dominate and probably destroy. Pan pulls voice forward, and with voice comes Psyche's inner power focused on an external world. Pan pulls Psyche's voice forward in the form of weeping, and Psyche's resolve dissolves into tears. Her wisdom, however, does not so dissolve. She grasps that Aphrodite's manipulation and will have brought her this low. She realizes that It has been Aphrodite's wisdom in collision with her own thinking that has brought the transformations that she now feels so keenly.

Pan tells Psyche that she must pray to Cupid because he will understand what has happened to them both. Ironic, yes, to cure Cupid's wounds, Psyche must ask Cupid for his help. The ancient author of this twist in the myth deeply understood the role that confession and forgiveness play in social healing, and knew that a public – or at least publically acknowledged – appeal for forgiveness (regardless of the basis for the appeal) can pave the way for yet other transformations.

In the myth of Psyche and Aphrodite, Cupid is the god of "relationships," though clearly at an external – and some would say superficial – fashion. Still, there isn't much of a future for those who would shun community "relationships." Dialogue in all its forms strives to explicitly impose at least some of Cupid's superficial rules of relationship; no personal attacks, for example. Structured dialogic design goes further in insisting that ideas cannot be attacked either, because ideas are an extension of a person. Without respect for community relationships, the goddesses cannot emerge.

Psyche cannot simply walk into a corner and start praying to Cupid. She first must find him so that he will hear her prayers. To find him, Psyche has to seek Aphrodite's help. Awkward, no? Psyche's mother-in-law – or is it ex-mother-in-law – doesn't like Psyche and isn't in the mood to be helpful. Cupid is in his mother's power, wounded from his marriage with Psyche, and a failure in the eyes of his mother. Psyche goes from god to goddess seeking help first from everyone else, and discovers that they all do not want to offend prevailing wisdom. Only then does Psyche face Aphrodite directly.

Aphrodite has her fun belittling Psyche. It is to be expected. However, to be recognized as a just and fair goddess, Aphrodite assigns Psyche four tasks if she chooses to seek redemption and gain Aphrodite's permission to speak to Cupid. Psyche's bargain is that if she fails in anyone of the tasks she will withdraw forever. The four tasks represent what we might agree to call "the way of the goddess" – naïveté, problem, waiting, and solution.

Psyche's acceptance depends upon a demonstration of her power to protect herself and her family from the dangers of inner words, moods, excesses, and illusions. The first task involved an impossible feat of sorting a complex hill of seeds into clusters based upon shared features. This was a task for discovering sameness. The seeds were like ideas from many sources. Psyche is overwhelmed by the complexity and falls within herself, contemplating suicide once again. Zeus (who acts from afar) seems to have sensed Psyche's plight and seems in sympathy with Psyche in the struggle of new wisdom with established wisdom. He sends help in the form of intelligent ants. Psyche accepts the help and with the help of the ants sorts the seeds as required.

As a commentary beyond the literal myth, Psyche has learned something about engaging complexity by sorting piles of ideas with help from others. She has also learned that each individual can do only so much when dealing with complexity alone. The seeds themselves are more understandable now that they have been sorted, and the pile of seeds itself has been organized into dimensions of complexity that are based on features shared by different types of seeds. Discovering the dimensions of the problem would not have been possible without the sorting. Aphrodite begrudgingly accepts that the first task indeed has been done.

Psyche's second task involves harvesting Golden Fleece from a fierce herd of rams who guard their lands ferociously. If she fails to return by nightfall, she must submit to death. Once more Psyche contemplates suicide, and once again Zeus sends help. Winds whispering through reeds at the edge of pond tell Psyche to gather wool that the rams leave behind at the end of the day after they have brushed up against brambles and branches of small trees. Psyche gathers the wool in this fashion and succeeds. Rather than digging into the coats of the rams and extracting their treasures, Psyche looks for what the rams have left behind in the form of their treasures. Psyche waits until the rams are through for the day and then gatherers her harvest.

Beyond the myth, Psyche gathers meanings from the symbolic statements made by the rams when she allows the rams time to complete their statements. By showing that she can gather authentic meaning from difficult beasts, Psyche succeeds and carries the statements faithfully back to Aphrodite. Aphrodite again must accept that the task has been done. In structured dialogic design, Psyche's second task finds a parallel in the clarification of ideas that follows the expression of labels for ideas. The process of jumping into clarification of ideas before all ideas have been gathered can anger some of the participants in a dialogue because they may fear that their clarification will be overlooked, forgotten, or misunderstood. It is the way of the goddess that will prevent this from happening.

Psyche's third task is an expression of Aphrodite's desire to put an end to this new wisdom. Psyche is told to fetch a glass of water from the river Styx. Those who know this river recognize that it cannot be approached with any measure of safety at all. Its very banks prevent any foot holds, and its turbulent water is guarded by dangerous monsters. The audience is not surprised when once again, Psyche collapses in tears and when Zeus sends help. Zeus sends an eagle, the eagle brings a glass over the river and lowers it down to catch some water, and Psyche returns once again triumphant.

Now there is a bit more here then what meets the eye. The river, and all water for that matter, is the unformed presence of wisdom. Special waters represent the wisdom of the gods and other waters the wisdom of the earth. When Psyche was sent to fetch a glass of wisdom from a primordial source of earthly waters, she found that she could not do this task alone. The solution is almost too simple. The eagle, with its unique airborne perspective, sees the means of carrying the river's wisdom to Psyche. The glass itself becomes a framework for carrying the wisdom as the wisdom took shape to fill the glass. Wisdom is harvested in the shape that is prepared to receive it. Wisdom cannot be taken in its raw form; it must be received in some structure.

The earthly wisdom and the goddess wisdom are not the same.

Psyche could not individually reach inside herself and fill a glass with her own tears to harvest the wisdom Aphrodite was demanding. At this point, Psyche has learned that when ideas are sorted and complexity is clarified, wisdom is harvested by yet another means. In structured dialogic design, the wisdom of a group is harvested at a point when a group is able to make pair wise comparisons among ideas essential for addressing their situations. The comparisons result in a framework, or a vessel, for holding the group's collective wisdom. Such wisdom can come from no one living source, but must be gathered up from within a pooled source.

Aphrodite is really displeased by Psyche's persistent successes. The fourth task involves a very dangerous pilgrimage. Psyche is to descend into the underworld and return with an impossible gift from the very queen of the underworld. So, does Psyche once again toss herself into a pile of transformational tears? No, but she does once again contemplate suicide.

Zeus somehow is not allowed to interfere this time. Psyche finds help in a surprising way. As she stands in a tower from which she intends to throw herself to her death, she hears the tower speak to her. The tower is the voice of the culture within which Psyche as a mortal princess has lived. The tower provides details, and supplies, and above all, a measure of hope. Psyche will bring honey cakes to distract beasts, coins to pay ferry passage, and humility to survive temptations.

Psyche sets out on her trip into the underworld, finds her way through the pathless path, descends to the river Styx, denies her urges to be helpful to those with other quests around her, catches her ferry ride, distracts the beasts, and is halfway done when she meets the queen of the underworld. Persephone, goddess of the underworld, greets Psyche warmly and offers lavish hospitality. Psyche has been forewarned that accepting the invitation into Persephone's culture will bind her to that culture forever, and keeps her distance in humble posture. With what by now must be imagined as a sense of unearthly confidence, Psyche asks Persephone for a gift of her beauty ointment – apparently a salve which prevents aging.

Persephone gives Psyche a cask, and Psyche dutifully begins her trip home.

All does go well, for a while. However, thinking how precious the cask must be as a means of preserving Aphrodite's colossal beauty, Psyche becomes tempted to claim some of it for her own – perhaps to win fair Cupid's heart anew. Opening the cask, Psyche is overcome with a deathly, ageless sleep. Though close now to home, she collapses as a victim of her own unknowing hand on the pathway homeward. Cupid just happens to have gotten over his hurt, and hears Psyche's final cry as she fell. He flies to her, and wakes her with the prick of one of his arrows. Cupid tells Psyche to continue home with the cask, and Cupid then flies to Zeus to proclaim his love for Psyche.

We needn't go into the love-hate dynamics between Zeus and Aphrodite, but the audience will intuitively know why he convenes all the gods and goddesses of the heavens to insist that Cupid formally marry the mortal Psyche. To get around the difficulties of a god marrying a mortal, Zeus gives Psyche a pot of immortality to drink and thereby formally anoints her emergence as a goddess. Aphrodite, we presume, is still fuming.

This fourth task is rich for those of us who practice dialogue management (even as we hold no aspiration for divine recognition). When a culture is ready, it will make it possible – though not easy – to access its secret treasures for wholesome purposes. In the process of serving the request to bring unvoiced treasures into the wisdom of the day, a temptation will exist to claim some measure of the treasure for oneself. Such a failing can be a fatal flaw, and without the love of others to save one from oneself, the success of the mission is very much in doubt. The goddess must be invited to walk a path to her own emergence. It is a dangerous path, and the goddess – like democracy itself – can be easily enslaved or slain. The goddess must be sustained with authentic love, and Cupid's return restores the sense of love for Psyche and the sensibility of love for the audience as well.

Storyboarding Emotion's Impact on Cognition

In all of us who would help others find our futures through dialogue, we can expect contact with Psyche and Zeus, Aphrodite and Cupid, and very much more. The magic of the myths is that they allow us all to pour ourselves into their stories. And also to understand their messages in the way that we conduct our lives.

Chapter Seven: Return of the Goddess –
Where is the Goddess in Modern Dialogue?

"But Goddess has never died, and one of the major spiritual and psychological phenomena of our time has been her reemergence as a significant presence in our lives. She has founded a central place in several of the great worlds religions – particularly, Catholicism and Hinduism. Goddess has been revived in modern cults, the spiritual ancestors of which are the earth cults of Demeter, Isis, and Asherah. She has made herself known in the metaphors, the myths, of modern science – particularly, psychology and climatology. She has expressed herself politically and sociologically in the drive for a new wholeness – a new spiritual, psychological, and physical ecology – that is the power behind what we call the women's movement. Goddess is returning because she is needed."

– ascribed as a biblical reference to the reemergence of <u>a Babylonian-like church (www.fresh-hope.com/forums/showthread.php?t=6227)</u>

The return of the Goddess that so many new agers talk about simply means a return of feminine power to the Earth. We all need to learn to be receptive to, and flow with Nature, rather than resisting it like we have for ages. This resistance has been a strictly masculine approach.

– http://www.gaia-back-to-the-garden.com/quotes-about-women.html

Gods, Goddesses, and Dialogue

The god and goddess theme isn't a gender thing. It speaks more to religious institutions founded on a supreme deity versus institutions within which a plurality of deities interact to shape the future of the universe. Ancient religions felt many sources of spiritual presence. The world was influenced by a plurality of interdependent divine forces. Modern, monotheistic religions rely on a dominant deity for governance [the paradox of the Christian trinity is the unity of a plurality of images of divinity within a single divine presence, but we are really not trying to open a profoundly theological discussion here]. For the purposes of contrasting institutional embodiments of religion, duality is personified in the commanding influence of a "god" in his hierarchical and distant power looking down upon the world – and plurality is personified in consensual influences of a "goddess" in her pervasive and imminent presence working through the world. The two world views do coexist.

The philosophical beheading offered up by Descartes fits tightly into the god view of his time.

Western Europe of the early 17th century easily accepted hierarchical partitioning as a part of the world order. The beheading was foreshadowed in fair measure by accepted belief in the legitimacy and inevitability of command and control governance. Seasons of democracy notwithstanding, hierarchical command was compelling. Cultural experience teaches that as families grow into clans, and clans into tribes, and tribes into bands, and bands into nations, leadership becomes progressively concentrated in individuals who are held apart from the "average" individual. Moments of democratic input are called upon for dealing with unusual challenges; and thereafter routine governance defaults to administrative management. Administrative managers enjoy elevated status. They are, to borrow from Descartes, heads of state – disembodied from the sacred hoi poloi – "the many."

We personify leaders as popular gods to legitimize hierarchical governance. It is not a gender thing. In the absence of a free, neutral and persistent press, modern heads of state hold elevated positions of distinction based on birthright, superior reasoning power, prowess in sports or combat, beauty or celebrity, or any other trait that can be a catalyst for influencing others. Do we oversimplify here? Perhaps. We do realize that each of us makes distinctions by setting up dualities for comparative purposes. We recognize that functioning systems – human systems through ecosystems – are understood by virtue of seeing the interconnections and interdependencies among parts. Parts within systems, however, can be illusion too. To see the forest, we must also see the trees. One tree in a forest is not all trees in the forest – nor is it any specific one tree. Each natural object is unique unto itself – distinct – yet unable to exist if alone. If we look closely at even a single atom, we find a cascade of interdependent subatomic particles. The point is that if we choose to find independent solid objects in a hierarchical "godly" world, we can imagine them. If we seek to see interdependencies linked in an integrated "godessly" world, we can find them too. Moving between a godly view of the world and the worldview of the goddess requires a transformative dialogue.

Opening a Transformative Dialogue

When we are asked a question and when we take time to think before we respond, we reach into ourselves to match the meaning of the question with what feels like an important idea to contribute as a response. Our response flows from our Body Wisdom. How do we grasp this importance? How do we feel it? As we fish the waters of our cognitive wisdom, what comes to the surface and leaps out? The term for this emergent presence of any one idea in an ocean of alternatives is called the idea's saliency.

How does an idea push itself forward? What manner of deep wisdom causes its upwelling? If we are asked to summon forth four or five of these leaping ideas, why are they sitting so near the surface of our consciousness? Our view is that body wisdom pulls and churns the seas of ideas while we sleep as well as while we are awake, and this churning is driven by unresolved felt questioning about complex situations. Body wisdom moves some of our silent ideas to the surface. When asked, what are the significant ideas that come to your mind (in response to a question about a problem situation that you are experiencing), we summon body wisdom to push those ideas forward for the group. In this way, individuals who silently draw from their own wells of understanding give voice to important, and perhaps also urgent, salient ideas.

In structured dialogue sessions, participants respond to a trigger question by jotting down their salient ideas on a piece of paper. Jotting their ideas down holds them in place on paper and provides some relief from the urgency that they may represent. Participants are calmed because they sense that body wisdom has spoken and their cognitive wisdom is tracking the results. The voyage has begun.

Individual participants then rewrite their notes to express each of their ideas in a single terse statement that captures the essence of the idea. This causes participants to reflect more closely on word choice, and as they fish through their cognitive resources once again, body wisdom is expressed in the form of word choices that have been pushed upward to salient positions.

As the participants in an SDD dialogue construct labels for their ideas, they are urged to be certain that the idea is a SINGLE idea. If a label relates to multiple ideas, they use their cognitive wisdom to break the idea down into single ideas (and this is important so that single ideas can be related to each other directly). This "digitizes" meaning in a fashion that makes finding connections among ideas easier.

Groups and communities are sometimes confronted with complex situations. Such unexplored situations have historically been referred to as problematiques, and recent authors have been calling them "wicked problems." They are poorly understood in terms of their parts; their parts continually change, and they continually interact with each other. Intervention focused on only one part leads to unintended consequences elsewhere in the system. The image on the next page illustrates steps that are used in the structured dialogic design (SDD) process as a problem solving tool.

To explore the high level of complexity of a problematique, group and community leaders need to sense the problem and then to arrive at a trigger question. With a clear view of what needs to be asked, community leaders then assemble an appropriate group to represent the diverse perspectives on the problem. A trigger question is used to elicit statements about the problem, which are captured as observations within the dialogue. Meanings behind the stated observations are clarified and then clustered in relationships of similarity.

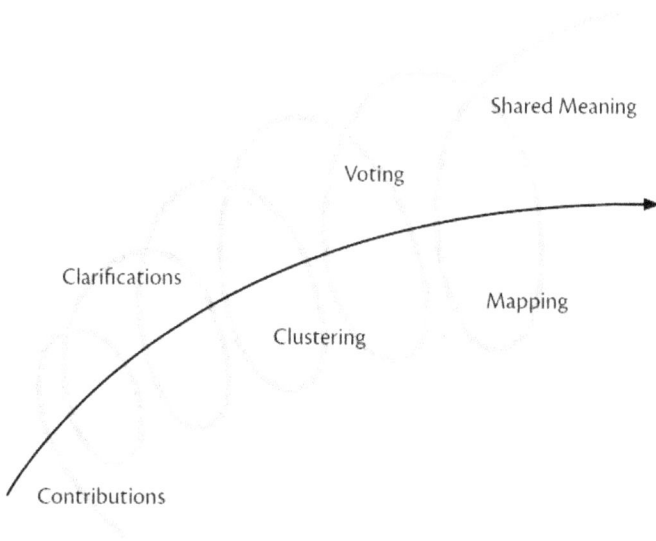

(source: Laouris, Underwood, Laouri & Christakis)

Participants in the dialogue construct the clusters and name them to help the group keep track of the meaning that they are sharing.

Once understandings and similarity relationships have been shared, participants express preference votes for constructing a systems view of their situation. Highly preferred observations are used to construct the initial systems view. The systems view is examined to reveal how unstructured preferences can lead otherwise to erroneous priorities when planning action to address the group's situation.

Systems learning is captured in the form of a new "story" which focuses on how important ideas, concerns, considerations or barriers relate to each other in an inclusive fashion. A second stage of dialogue focuses on the exploration of action options, the construction of action scenarios, and the selection of a consensus action plan. Action planning benefits from the discovery of a strongly held view of the situation facing the group along with the culture of collaboration that develops in the group.

The structured dialogic design process – as an integrated approach to complex dialogues – pushes us toward faith in our better selves, hope for peace with our environment, and charity in respect and collaboration with each other. This is what we have been seeking to say when we state that body wisdom pushes us along three vectors originating from the core of our being, building harmony among ourselves, and finding our balance with our surroundings.

Evoking the Goddess

Body Wisdom plays an essential role in all of the phases of dialogue in the SDD process. In broad terms, body wisdom helps us discern when we need to engage an important problem. Even with this wisdom, we can expect to face challenges in raising a specific community problem to the top of the list of community concerns. It is generally the case that community leaders need to engage a problem well before they can hope to completely understand it, and engaging the unknown takes a measure of courage. For some leaders and for some types of complex problems, engaging the unknown can seem impossible. It is an act of hope – if not of faith – to begin exploring a complex problem with serious implications in a highly public way. The challenge can be reduced if the community has a history of working well together with complex situations. Trust can be kindled if even a small portion of a community's leadership has had successful experience working through complexity in large groups. The *go or no-go* decision that community leaders take will be framed by a sense of necessity or urgency, the level of trust in the community, and prior experience in working with complex problems through open and focused dialogue. Truly complex problems tend to ferment when kept away from the light of day.

When a complex situation is explored with a dialogue process such as SDD, it is highly likely that some individuals in the community who have essential perspectives to share may never have met or worked with others who are convened into the group. To bring key people together around a complex problem, an environment of highly visible respect and trust has to be established early in the process. Trust is first cultivated with the style in which invitations are extended and recruitment is managed.

There are options for how to proceed. Core parts of an SDD dialogue are also found in other respectful dialogue approaches. After the formal process of idea clarification, relationships among distinct (digitized) ideas are explored with clustering. This is step is becoming increasingly used across dialogue methods. Participants in SDD, however, uniquely apply a systems mapping step to structure digitized ideas and define root causes or deep opportunities.

In any large group collaborative planning process, it is possible that emphasis can be inappropriately focused on the mechanics of information management. It is through the social process of inclusive and harmonious planning that authentic and enduring value is created in the community. The process can be transformative, if even limited to specific cycles of necessity. Not all community problem solving and management decisions could or should be addressed with large group dialogue. From the preface to this book we have heard that indigenous people used large group dialogue specifically when a problem existed for which no single individual had a clear understanding of what actions to take. Large group processes such as SDD are a means of understanding a complex process and also recruiting community members into a collaborative response to those problems. A spirit of inclusive involvement is the most prized outcome of an appropriately managed collaborative design. The design must be rational in the minds and hearts of all participants, yet even though this rationality is essential it is not in itself sufficient to mobilize a community.

Large group events need to be as mindful of how they close as they have been with respect to how they begin. A ritualized closing that is used in SDD is the telling of the new story. This is done with "readings" of the systems map that the group has constructed. The new narrative is a shared creative gift that the group gives to each other. It is metaphorically like the birth of a new understanding through the ministration of the goddess. The event does not end with the production of a document that then sits on a shelf, but instead moves onward into the community through the re-telling that members of the group share with others. A successful community dialogue should radiate into the larger community. Participants who experience the goddess in dialogue should feel comfortable carrying the spirit of the goddess back into the community with them. The new narrative is a means of fostering this radiance.

Participants in SDD dialogues experience a powerful co-creative process within which they take on a communal personality. Without stepping firmly into theological territory, we assert that the group's special quality is a manifestation of a presence that is larger than the collection of participants themselves. Some might interpret this collective group consciousness in the context of a "super-organism" ... but we are content to say that the group evokes the presence of the goddess. We are not going to assert that SDD is the only way – though we do feel it is the most agile and consistently effective way – to evoke the presence of the goddess. We will leave the final verdict, of course, to the readers and to those who have grappled with complexity using dialogue processes like SDD throughout the world.

A Final Word

We cannot conclude our discussion of the link between body wisdom and cognitive wisdom without once again appealing to the humanity of Albert Einstein: "*The intuitive mind is a sacred gift and the rational mind is a faithful servant. We have created a society that honors the servant and has forgotten the gift.*" While Einstein might be most remembered for his mathematical persistence and genius, we can confidently say that he should be thanked for his sense of balance. His genius carries the touch of the goddess.

Some Selected References

Bausch, K.C (2010). *Body* Wisdom – *Interplay of Body and Ego.* Ongoing Emergence Press, Riverdale GA

Bausch, K.C. 2001) *The Emerging Consensus in Social Systems Theory.* Plenum, NY

Christakis A.N and Bausch, K.C. (2006). *How People Harness their Collective Wisdom and Power to Construct the Future in Co-Laboratories of Democracy.* Information Age Publishing.

Delbecq A. L. and VandeVen A. H, (1971). "A Group Process Model for Problem Identification and Program Planning," *Journal Of Applied Behavioral Science* VII (July/August, 1971), 466 -91.

Delbecq, A.L., (1967) The Management of Decision-Making within the Firm – Three Types of Decision-Making, *Academy Management Journal*, December, pp. 322-339.

Flanagan, T.R. and Bausch K.C. (2011) *A Democratic Approach to Sustainable Futures* Ongoing Emergence Press, Riverdale GA

Flanagan, T.R. and Christakis, A.N. (2010). *The Talking Point: Creating an Environment for Exploring Complex Meaning.* Information Age Publishing.

Johnson, R.A. (1989) *She: Understanding Feminine Psychology.* Harper Perennial, New York, NY.

Shank, G. Modes of Peircean Abduction www.cs.indiana.edu/event/maics96/Proceedings/shank.html. EPCSE Dept., Northern Illinois University.

About the Authors and Illustrator

Tom Flanagan was raised in Massachusetts and attended universities in Massachusetts and Connecticut. He began his professional career in life science working in biomedical technology companies in New England and in Europe. Tom's interests in decision-making in diversified R&D teams led him to advanced studies at the MIT Sloan School of Management, and then to the opportunity to work with Dr. Alexander N. Christakis in co-laboratories of democracy within international businesses, communities and government agencies.

Tom has taught classes in biology, chemistry, engineering, and management at the University of Massachusetts and has worked with online teams and classes in participatory democracy.

His published books include *The Talking Point: Creating an Environment for Exploring Complex Meaning*, (with AN Christakis; Information Age

Publishing, Inc., Charlotte, NC, 2010), *A Democratic Approach to Sustainable Futures* (with KC Bausch: Emergence Press, Riverdale, GA, 2011), and *Body Wisdom in Dialogue* (with KC Bausch: Ongoing Emergence Press, Riverdale, GA, 2012).

Kenneth C. Bausch, PhD, grew up in Ohio and received his BA in Philosophy from Duns Scotus College followed by four years of intensive theological studies at St. Leonard's College. He began his professional life as a Catholic priest of the Franciscan Order and has been a pastor, a high school teacher, an inner-city organizer working with street gangs and community groups, a counselor, a social service administrator, a real estate agent, a homebuilder, a contractor, a university professor, a research director, and an organizational consultant. In the course of 40 years of inquiry into the human condition, he has delved intensively into philosophy, orthodox theology, Eastern religions, social and political ideology, psychology, sociology, and systems theory. Ken also holds an MA in Psychology at West Georgia University and a Ph.D. in Psychology from Saybrook University. After a brief stint as Executive Director at the Ashley Montague Institute in Lo Angeles, Ken took up the leadership role of the Institute for 21st Century Agoras.

Ken has taught psychology, sociology and systems science at Mercer University, Perimeter College, DeVry Institute, and Capella University) and is currently teaching an online course through Flinders University in Australia. His published books include *The Emerging Consensus in Social Systems Theory,* (Kluwer Academic/Plenum Press; 2001), *Harnessing Collective Wisdom and Power to Construct the Future* (with Aleco Christakis; Information Age Publishing, Greenwich, CT, 2006). *Body Wisdom: Interplay of Body and Ego* (2010) and (with Tom Flanagan) *A Democratic Approach to Sustainable Futures* (2011) and *Body Wisdom in Dialogue* (Ongoing Emergence Press, Riverdale, GA, 2012).

Yuu Asano caught the attention of the authors *of Body Wisdom in Dialogue* with illustrations which appeared in a 2008 report by Professor Jacqueline Wasilewski of International Christian University (ICU) in Tokyo, Japan, entitled "Creating Global *Agoras* & Other *MIID* Communities." The authors immediately recognized that Yuu had the artistic consciousness and skilled hand that could carry their thoughts and feelings into graphic expression.

Yuu began translating ideas into graphics as part of her undergraduate academic work at ICU where she was one of Professor Wasilewski's advisees in intercultural communication, while simultaneously pursuing studies as a Japanese/English simultaneous interpreter.

Like some of the great poets, Yuu can "translate" sound into other senses. Time and time again her synesthetic talent of turning words into color and shape enabled students from diverse backgrounds speaking multiple languages to reach mutual understanding. It is fascinating to watch her work. It is like watching someone "draw" an "essay," giving, not only words, but abstract concepts, color, form, in short, physical substance. It is a totally fluid process. Her works can also be found as "mind mappings" and "graphic facilitations."

About the AGORAS

The Institute for 21st Century Agoras (AGORAS), an international nonprofit education enterprise incorporated in the State of California in June 2002, is a membership organization composed of university-affiliated, independent, and corporate social system dialogue managers who promote participatory democracy through the practice of authentic, large group, collaborative design. By corporate charter, the AGORAS will:

- Promote the idea of human connectedness and interdependence (the "global village")
- Promote democratic processes for addressing the problems and opportunities associated with global economic and political integration
- Promote the establishment of co-laboratories of democracy

The AGORAS maintains archives of field applications contributed from individuals who use structured dialogic design for democratic social system services.

INSTITUTE for 21st
CENTURY AGORAS

info@globalagoras.org   www.globalagoras.org

www.ingramcontent.com/pod-product-compliance
Lightning Source LLC
Chambersburg PA
CBHW072250270326
41930CB00010B/2328